DON'T GET
ME STARTED

DON'T GET ME STARTED

Kate Clinton

BALLANTINE BOOKS
THE BALLANTINE PUBLISHING GROUP
NEW YORK

A Ballantine Book
Published by The Ballantine Publishing Group

Copyright © 1998 by Kate Clinton

http://www.randomhouse.com

Library of Congress Cataloging-in-Publication Data
Clinton, Kate.
Don't get me started / Kate Clinton. — 1st ed.
p.   cm.
ISBN 0-345-38887-9 (alk. paper)
1. Clinton, Kate.   2. Comedians—United States—Biography.
3. Lesbians—United States—Biography.   I. Title.
PN2287.C5455A3   1998
792.7′028′092—dc21

[B]   98-4801
                                                         CIP

Text design by Holly Johnson

Manufactured in the United States of America

First Edition: June 1998

10 9 8 7 6 5 4

For Urvashi
my literal one

Contents

CONTENTS

our chip site—www.laugh.orgorgorgorg

Introduction

It is a crazy cockamamie world out there. And I mean no insult to the memory of Mamie Eisenhower. I lived most of my single digits during the Eisenhower years. Those years that got Betty Friedan so steamed. She must have been taking notes while I was being raised in upstate New York, middle child in a middle-class, sporting, Irish Catholic family. Three brothers, one sister. My parents were married forty-two years; they knew each other fifty-two. I must have been taking notes on what were to be the themes of my comic life.

Until I was ten years old we lived outside Buffalo, New York, where my parents grew up. My mother's father worked on the Erie railroad, a traveling machinist with his own boxcar toolshop. He often drew the floor plans of his workspace for me. My favorite childhood book was *The Boxcar Children*. I became susceptible to a life of travel.

He was tough and Irish Catholic and was often chased by the Ku Klux Klan in South Buffalo on his way home from work. When he was young he was a partier, but I knew him as a formal Trumanesque figure in white linen summer suits or pinstriped three-piece suits with suspenders and vest pocket watches at Sunday dinners. He made diluted crème de menthe parfaits. He had a small study in my grandparents' flat where I excused myself, after the parfaits, and played the colored 45 rpms he collected for us. "Teddy Bear's Picnic." "If you go down to the woods today, you better not go alone." I knew I would need a road manager.

At Sunday dinners, I sat next to my grandfather. At some point during the meal he would get a piece of food stuck on his lip, some sticky crumb of something, and I would look, in wide-eyed horror at the wabi on his perfection. I could not tell him of his food gaffe. Finally, my grandmother would say, "Will! For heaven's sake! Wipe your mouth."

During dessert he waited for me to eat the white creamy frosting I had saved for last and remarked, "Now will you look at that?" I'd look. And he would eat my frosting. Every Sunday. I learned irony and indirection.

My grandmother was cool and formal. She really let down in her eighties when she was in the nursing home. When my mother and I visited her there, she would look at my mom and ask her when she was going to get married. I would look at my mother and wait archly for the answer. I learned how to be a straight man.

By the end of her life, my grandmother's favorite word was "baby" and she used it as a noun, a verb, and an adjective in wild careening sentences. "The baby baby babied the baby down the baby and baby baby baby." My mother lived in fear that in her older years she would fixate on a word that was not as nice as baby. I looked forward to that day when my mother, who only said "darnation" when vexed, would swear like a stevedore. I learned about getting bleeped.

My father's side of the family was wild and much more interesting, so we never got to see them enough. They lived in a two-family house blocks away from my mother's family. They all smoked and drank and carried on. My dad's father had died when he was six. My grandmother had to take in boarders. Strangers were always entering and exiting. Some stayed and talked. One was her man friend, Bill, a big retired day laborer. I loved the sound of his job. Day laborer. There was always a mutt, always named Bunny, tap-dancing, skittering on the old linoleum, yelping through the downstairs and upstairs flat, paying no attention to everyone yelling, "Bunny, down!" I learned chaos.

My dad's only and older sister, Kathryn, lived in the upstairs flat and was as close to a flapper as I've ever seen. The smell of boiled cabbage mixed with that of her fingernail polish. She was always doing her red fingernails and had her coarse gray hair up in a couple of pink spoolies because they were "goin' out for a fish fry then dancin'." I never heard her use a "g." I learned glamour and conspiracy.

Her husband, Uncle Ev, had "a good job at the bank" but he quit it because "he thought he was too good for it," to become a ticket taker at the War Memorial during the winter and a bet taker at the racetrack windows during the summer. "He went from one set of bars to another." He was the prototype for Archie Bunker. When I saw him in his casket, it was the first time I had ever seen him without a cigar in his mouth.

His passion was racing pigeons. After visiting my mother's family for Sunday dinner, we stopped to see my dad's side of the family on the way out of town, "just for half an hour." That was usually the half hour that my uncle's pigeons, his beloved birds, would be coming home, just ahead of him, as he roared down the street, yelling to my aunt, "Kate! Get those sheets down."

My father worked for thirty-three years for an upstate New York power and light company. In answer to the rhetorical question meant to guilt trip you into turning off the lights, "Whad yer father do, work for the power company?" I could always answer yes. He began working summers during college digging holes for new electricity poles. In fluted, curling black-and-white pictures he is tanned, ruggedly handsome. He went to college on a football scholarship. He was nicknamed "Stone-crusher."

His support of his mother and young family and his poor vision kept him out of World War II. Instead he took care of all the wives and families of his friends who had enlisted. He worked up through the power company, from outside work to data processing to personnel management. When he had to give a speech, he dreaded it but I helped him. He would raise his eyebrows at any off-color joke I told at dinner, but then I would hear that he had used it at a company luncheon.

My mother taught kindergarten until she married my father and had her own. Five children in twelve years. She said she wanted ten. She was a constant mother. She sewed, did laundry, and baked every day. She prided herself on her hooked rag rugs. She said the one in their room was so tightly wound, not even a spiked heel could go through. Not that anyone in my parents' bedroom was wearing spiked heels. To the best of my knowledge.

She attended daily mass, visited the sick in the parish, and prayed mightily. She gardened, loved to play bridge, and was a rabid fan at any of her kids' sporting events. Sometimes on a Friday night, not in Lent, she and my father split a beer. She did volunteer work at an inner-city Montessori school. My mother ironed her way through the McCarthy and Watergate hearings. She loved Richard Nixon and hated Betty Friedan.

She and I played the "Hell Toupee" game. We spotted rugs so bad, a spiked heel could easily pierce them, but we also prided ourselves on the more subtle detection of fake hair well done. Unfortunately, she died before hair plugs. She had an untapped wicked streak and often got hysterical during stories of one tragedy after another. She would try to make it look as if she were crying, but I knew better.

In high school my best friend's mother, Jane, was my comic mother. She had more leisure time than my own mother and a knack for found humor. She got a Frederick's of Hollywood catalog years before anyone else and did dramatic readings. She'd also call and say, "Channel Four, right now," and hang up. I'd turn on the TV and there would be Bette Midler for the first time on Merv Griffin. We listened to Moms Mabley, Richard Pryor, and Mike Nichols and Elaine May.

My mother told us that God had a plan for us, that each of us was special. Our family vacations were spent tracking God's plan and my older brothers' vocations. I went to Catholic school from elementary through college and was heavily recruited for the convent. I thought the Maryknoll missionaries were very glamorous and I loved their little hand-sized publication, and while I certainly had the face and the calves for it, I never did hear the call of a vocation.

In elementary school I was a chronic overachiever. In second grade, during the Thanksgiving unit, in the time it took my classmates to glue one feather on a construction paper headband, I had created an entire Native village with life-sized teepee, a strap-on over-the-shoulder canoe, a sweat lodge, and a fire pit with flames made of red cellophane. I learned to be overprepared.

In high school I wrote compositions that brought the class to tears or laughter. Math and physics destroyed my average. Each night before cheerleader try-outs I sprained my ankle so I didn't ever have to try out. Instead, I formed the pep club and was in charge of a huge basketball pep rally the day that John F. Kennedy was assassinated.

In the late sixties I went to a small Jesuit college in upstate New York, lived at home with my parents and younger brother and sister, and worked part-time. Student protests against the Vietnam war were shutting down colleges throughout the country. I thought my radical classmates were annoying and immature. I didn't want to lose my hard-earned tuition money. I was cautious, conservative, pre–Michael J. Fox. It might have been different if I had done the drugs, but I had to go home and face my parents each night.

My major was English with a minor in Education. At that time, on the cusp of feminism, the job options for women were nursing and teaching and since I don't do bodily functions, I decided to teach English.

It was before the advent of Women's Studies so in English classes I wondered what was so quintessentially

American about hunting a great white whale. Where was Mrs. J. Alfred Prufrock? The one time I theorized that *The Aenead* was really about Dido and should therefore be called *The Didead*, my paper was read out loud to the bemusement of my class and I was told to rewrite it. When we read *Madame Bovary*, my professor wondered Socratically about what Emma might be thinking and would call on me with "Let's get it from the horse's mouth."

My senior Ethics professor announced that homosexuality (the first and only time the word had been said in class) was nothing more than mutual masturbation (ditto for that word). That set me back, although years later we were both Grand Marshals in the New York City Gay Pride Parade. Do I dare to eat a peach? Yes. But I get ahead of myself.

Teaching high school English was the hardest work I ever did. After eight years, I had to leave. To qualify for a leave of absence, I got a friend of mine, Rita Speicher, to vouch that I would be attending the writing school she directed. Since I had spent twenty-four of my twenty-nine years in school, I had no intention of going, but when I went to the introductory class I was hooked. The Women's Writers Center had operated for ten years in unused classrooms in a declining two-year college outside Syracuse, New York. Women from all over the country attended. Guest writers came for week-long seminars, taught, critiqued our writing, and spun out feminist theory.

I was on fire. I read all the women I had suspected were writing during those whale-hunting, peach-eating times waiting for the iceman to cometh. Susan Glaspell. Kate Chopin. H.D. Zora Neale Hurston. I read women thinkers and my tightly locked, Jesuit-educated mind had its doors blown off. But good. Mary Daly—*Beyond God the Father* and *Gyn/Ecology*, Susan Griffin—*Women and Nature*, Adrienne Rich—*The Dream of a Common Language* and *Women and Honor: Some Notes on Lying*, Muriel Rukeyser—*The Life of Poetry*. It was a very heady year.

It was more than heady. It was body-y. I, who had come out to myself, and then to and with another woman in my last months of teaching, came into a community of women. When I first went to the Writers Center I was completely intimidated. I had never been among lesbians. I didn't know from patchouli or processing. They thought I was a spy from the suburbs, a straight infiltrator. It could have been the Liz Claibornes. But the rip-roaring excitement of the ideas, the palpable eroticism of the life of an awakening mind was a great and immediate leveler. We read together, argued fiercely, drank tequila shooters, danced wildly, laughed hysterically, gossiped mercilessly. At times, I thought I might just blow up.

The year I attended the Writers Center the visiting writers were Susan Sherman, Olga Broumas, Marge Piercy, and finally Adrienne Rich. In the very first week Rita Mae Brown visited. I had no idea who she was, had never read *Rubyfruit Jungle*, but was completely enthralled by her sassy, fierce wit. As were my fellow classmates, who for the rest of the year imitated Rita Mae's style of wearing shirts unbuttoned to below the sternum. In upstate New York that meant an unending series of colds.

Because it was the Women's Writers Center, not the Women's Readers Center, I wrote. Poems; dreadful. I began a novel. I wrote short stories. We did public readings of our work. At local universities, at coffeehouses, at nursing homes. Only once at a nursing home. After four or five lugubrious poetry readings—"the light . . . my heart . . . the waves crashing . . . I hate my mother"—a voice from the back of the solarium piped up, "Pep it up, sweetie!"

By the end of most readings, our listeners wanted any excuse for release, and as cleanup reader in the lineup, I played my stuff for laughs, whether they were there or not. Eventually I began to think that I could write more directly for the laughs. Each time we had a visiting writer, I asked what she thought of women and humor. By the end of the year, I had perfected my question and asked Adrienne Rich why there was so little written about women and humor. She looked me right in the eye and said, "You write it." I took that as an order.

The next year I did not go back to my tenured teaching job. Instead, I started a freelance life of window washing, SAT tutoring, substitute teaching, and working on an essay about the uses of humor in the women's movement called "Making Light." When I showed it to my friend Susie, she asked, "Where are the jokes?" I had talked and talked and talked about trying stand-up until my best friend Deirdre got so sick of it, she booked me into a local club and said, "You are on in a month."

We hung up a poster in the club. I wrote the jokes. I contacted one hundred and eighty of my closest friends and on March 21, 1981, performed my first show. It was thirty-three minutes long. The audience, all trusted veteran codependents, laughed supportively.

The next day, as I laid out on the couch, supine from my comic efforts, my partner, Trudy Wood, said, "I don't know how to tell you this, but you're going to have to do this more than once." I was flabbergasted. I had never thought of performing beyond one time. I had just wanted to try it. My partner who in that moment became my manager, was, as usual, way ahead of me. The "Where are the jokes?" friend had been in a woman's rock band, Sweet Jenny Grit, that had broken up after ten years, so she volunteered to book me for the summer. She booked me for the next five years.

My second performance was in Boston, Massachusetts, in an old loft in the South End. Since I could not
bus all my close personal friends there—Boston has
never taken to bussing—I was colonically nervous.
Thirty-five of Boston's finest lesbians sprawled on old
cushions strewn throughout the space. They weren't
hostile. More politely wary. Without any reaction from
them I stumbled, but continued. I began to theorize
that perhaps you have to be sitting up to laugh.

In the classroom, I had faced sullen audiences and had
learned not to go into a blind, murderous panic and leave
if it was not going well, so I forged on. When the line that
had brought down the house in my first outing met a
leaden silence, I faltered again. From the back of the
room, came a voice in the purest South Boston accent,
"Y'er on yer own now, dahlin!" I still hear that voice.

On the drive home, in our red van named Ruby, as
in Fruit, I asked my booker, the ex-rocker, how long a
show should be. She thought for a bit and pronounced
that it should be a forty-five-minute set, with a break
and then another forty-five-minute set. I was vulnerable
enough to take directions, and she seemed so certain. I
went home and wrote a two-set show. Ninety minutes.
When I tell my comedian friends who spend years hon-
ing six or ten minutes of material for that vaunted spot
on late-night talk shows, they are amazed and amused.

The flowering of women's culture in the early 1980s

was such an underground phenomenon that it should more accurately be called "mushrooming." Women's mainstream culture in the 1990s set deep roots in that lesbian loam. I started there. I did not go the route of opener, middle, or headliner sets in the burgeoning comedy club scene. After all, I was talking about being a lesbian and it was the Reagan years. I could have changed pronouns and talked about kitties and doggies and peanuts on airplanes, but I didn't.

It wasn't a conscious choice. I never gave myself the assignment, "Today, let's write about lesbians." I just did it. And there was a lot to talk about. Coming out stories, dating rituals, softball teams, local lore, fashion. We were PI before PI was cool. I had no trouble filling ninety minutes.

Whenever I tried to write straighter material at the urging of my more commercially minded friends who thought that as a lesbian comedian, I had a sophisticated career death wish, I wrote the most arcane lesbiana. What is funniest is what is truest and I was interested in telling the truth about my life. I believed what the poet Muriel Rukeyser said, "When a woman tells the truth of her life, the world splits open."

By the mid-eighties the women's cultural network was changing. Four years of Reagan and economic necessity atomized the lesbian community. The women's distribution network dwindled from ninety distributors in local

towns to ten in huge territories. Coffeehouses closed. The
separatist community, so comforting, so defining, finally
proved to be too closed, too implosive a system.

Since 1980, I have kept notes on five-by-eight
cards—items from the news, a found phrase, ideas for
bits. Hundreds of cards, numbered, and dated. On card
#31 in June 1981, an article from *Newsweek* science
news—"gay cancer?" In the mid-eighties, lesbians and
gay men began working together, forced into coalition to
respond to the AIDS crisis and to the growing opposition
of the right wing. Anita Bryant proved to be a great orga-
nizer in the gay and lesbian community. I began to get
calls to speak at mixed gay and lesbian dinners and rallies. Some adventurous gay men began to come to my
shows. Bathroom lines at intermission were co-gendered.

In 1987, I emceed an hour of the rally at the March
on Washington. I marched until we passed the White
House, "Two, four, six, eight—how do you know that
Ronnie's straight?" and then left to go to the rally stage.
I had been in many gay pride parades, had once even
hitched a ride with the Dykes on Bikes in the San Francisco gay pride parade, and loved the sheer queer cele-
bratory, outrageous carnival atmosphere. My shortcut to
the rally stage took me to the AIDS Quilt, laid out at
dawn that morning. As I walked past rows and rows of
panels, past family and friends clustered, crying, panel
searching, holding each other, I was forever changed
into a more serious comic.

The new seriousness made me funnier. Perhaps a holdover from my mother's reaction to bad news. In Hindi, the word "rolla" means laughing and crying at the same time. I never bought the binary break between serious and humorous, that only serious can bear the weight of truth, that humorous is trivial, less than truthful. I became a full court rover.

Once, when my dad was visiting, we invited friends over for dinner and the only conversation rule I laid down ahead of time was no discussion of sex. That was for my benefit. My father sat and listened through dinner conversation of gay politics, gay theory, gay gossip, and toward the end of the discussion, I turned to my dad and asked, "Well, Mr. Clinton (we have a very formal relationship), what do you think we as gay people can do to make more bridges to straight people?" My dad did one of his patented, exquisitely timed pauses and replied, "Keep talking."

This book comes from the very rich if recent tradition of stand-up comics in publishing. It comes from the even rarer tradition of the comic, me, actually writing the book. For years a woman in Ohio urged me to write this book. I lost her address when she moved to Florida to have fun in the sun while I was slaving away over a hot Mac. I would like to find her and choke her.

Making the transition from the evanescent performed word with its pauses, hand gestures, and tones of voice to the substantial written word with its commas, parentheses, and speed of reading has been a challenge.

I wanted to call the book *There's a Joker in the Menstrual Hut* after those fabulous communal huts where tribal women go every twenty-eight days, give little back rubs, dish, sing songs. I always pictured the men outside holding the hands of small crying children, tapping on the hut, "Honey, you've been in there twenty-three days. We're almost out of casseroles." But my editors, worried about shelf life, predicted that the book would go from the women's health section to the remainder bins in a week or two.

I wanted to have a little computer chip laugh track in the back of the book that you could press if you didn't want to laugh alone. But apparently there have been some rogue computer chips that have gone off like a late-night car alarm and driven bookstore owners to distraction. And in today's mega bookstores you'd hate to draw attention to yourself, so my publisher nixed it, much to the disappointment of my seven-year-old niece. So here it is. Read it out loud to your friends. Stand up when you do it. Use hand gestures.

adjudiKate

1. judge not lest ye be Wapner.

A friend of mine was called for jury duty just before Christmas. She sat for a day and a half in the holding area until she was summoned for a criminal trial. She and her cohorts were ushered into an empty courtroom where the judge thanked them all in advance for their service in the busy holiday season. He reminded them that justice takes no holiday and encouraged them to think of jury duty in the same way that they think of military service: as an honor and privilege in the preservation of democracy.

When it came time for the one-on-one interview, my friend told the judge she was a lesbian. She said she would be excluded from serving in the military because of that. Using the military precedent, she argued that injustice should not get a holiday and that she should be dismissed. He said he got her point and excused her. My friend felt vindicated by this stunning appeal to juris logic.

Unfortunately, this same friend believes she can pass the law boards just by watching horsewoman Greta von Sustern on *Court TV*. For her, the O.J. trial, not the Scopes trial, the Rosenberg trial, or the Lindbergh trial, was the trial of the century. If all the coverage of the O.J. trial were laid end to end, it did last a century.

She watched O.J. all day, every day. We fought about the jury. It should have been six Mennonites, six Amish, all of them wondering, "What's a Bronco?" Jury pools should have been taken from homeless people. They don't have TVs. They'd have a place to stay, three square meals, something to do all day.

After the O.J. trial, people like her who had grown dependent on a daily *Court TV* fix, turned to cable. Luckily, our litigious ways have certainly picked up quantum speed in this century. The court of public opinion works many different circuits. The governmental: Watergate, the Anita Hill hearings, the Iran Contra hearings, the Single Sheik Theory, Whitewatergate, Oklahoma City. The mental: the unabomber, the nutbucket who defended himself in court in the New York commuter train shootings and questioned one victim, "Do you see the person who shot you in this court?" Commuter, "Yes, it was you." "Can you point him out?" "Yes, it was you." "I rest my case."

The personal: the Menendez Brothers; the Mac-Martins; Pete Rose, Mike Tyson, and Marv "The Biter" Albert in Sport Court. Despite intense coverage, many questions remain unanswered in the Bobbitt trial. How did Lorena end up in the car with it? Why did she panic and throw it out the car window, mercifully down at the time? What remorse caused her to notify the police, who went on a mission to find it, sweeping the field with metal detectors people use at the beach. (Every newspaper article noted, "they found it lying in the tall grass." That sounded so biblical. "And they picketh it up and laideth it in a Ziploc bag.")

Surprisingly, it turned out that a penis is not a pre-existing medical condition, so Howard Stern did a benefit for John Wayne's Bobbitt and his medical expenses. He raised $26,000, enough to reattach three penises. So they put one on Camille Paglia.

Courts have appeal. There are television shows: *Court TV* first with Judge Wapner, then with Judge Ed Koch. *LA Law. Judge Judy. Night Court.* There are movies. *To Kill a Mockingbird*—my early favorite courtroom drama. I loved Scout and I still think, on any windy tree-rustling night, that Boo Radley could jump out at me. *A Few Good Men.* And the women who love them. *Judge Dredd. The Verdict.* There are books. On airlines, so many passengers' faces are buried in John Grisham books, they could be complimentary copies for Grisham Airlines.

And through it all, we worried John Jr. would never pass the bar.

But for my money, the trial of the century was the obscenity trial of 2 Live Crew in Ft. Lauderdale, Florida, 1990. Granted, this late entry into the century sweepstakes did not have the flashiest of graphics, the sidebarial excitement, or even Rosa Lopez. But it did have its glorious moment.

It's not that I am a big follower of rap music or a big advocate of rap music lyrics. That would mean I could understand them and I don't. I have not understood most lyrics since Crystal Gale, poster child for Drano, sang, "Donuts make your brown eyes blue."

Though I can't tell the difference between Ice T and Run DMC or Heavy D, I can tell you who Tipper Gore is. Pound for pound, she is one of the cutest VP wives we've ever had. Her rap on rap lyrics got people all nutted up in Florida where apparently no one uses bad language, except if they are German and being carjacked, dragged out of their rental cars in the Orlando airport parking lot. "Gettn outen uvv mein farkin volksvagen, got dam gun toten juven tuten mayhem!"

Despite a NSO65 rating (No senator over 65) pasted in Day-Glo stickers on the albums, the 2 Live Crew merch was confiscated and the Crew was hauled into court. During the proceedings, the lyrics were read in a very lawyerly, very dry tone. Several times, the court reporter was asked to read them back. A steel-gray-haired button-down grown-up read in a flat-line monotone, without benefit of the driving backbeat, "I want to grab you from behind, grab your big ole butt and bam bam bam [throat clearing] la la la oooo baby oooo baby, et cetera." Thank you, that will be all.

After almost three days of testimony, the jury looked noticeably pained. During supervised breaks they were spotted in the hallways, cracking up, tears streaming down their faces, sliding helplessly down the wall by the water fountains. Finally the jury foreman passed a note to the judge: "The jurors have an unusual request. Some of them are experiencing physical pain. They want to know if they can laugh in your court." The judge sympathized with their efforts to remain stone-faced during the trial and presented their request. The lawyers offered no objection. The jurors were told they could laugh in court.

That moment ranks higher than the moment when the O.J. jury foreman announced the "not guilty" verdict or when John Bobbitt was acquitted of raping his wife for lack of evidence.

advoKate

1. not the magazine.

In the 1996 presidential election, Senator Bob Dole could have gotten an extra campaign boost if he'd hinted around that he was going to come out. "Bob Dole has a big announcement for the American people. The reason Bob Dole accepts campaign money from Gay Republicans is because Bob Dole is one." It was about the only thing he didn't do. Look what it did for Ellen DeGeneres's ratings. Forty-two million people tuned in to watch Ellen Morgan come out. If half of them had voted for the senator from Kansas, he'd have been elected.

For eight months on talk shows and in interviews, Ellen DeGeneres hinted that in her new season Ellen Morgan was going to come out. In some interviews she said Ellen Morgan was, pause, hint, hint, nudge, nudge,

wink, wink, Lebanese. She teased that the hints had
been there all along—the hummus, the Casey Kasem
references. Blond people in the Midwest were confused
and thought, funny, she doesn't look Lebanese. The
Middle East peace process was jeopardized.

Some of my friends thought Ellen's coming out was
going to change everything. One believed that calen-
dars hereafter would be measured B.E. and A.E. She
numbers 1997 as 1 A.E. and claims that Ellen's coming
out will usher in not only the end of homophobia, but
also the end of racism, sexism, and ageism. Big, big.

Ellen's coming out made other friends of mine,
jaded hohumasexuals, very impatient. Whenever I get
impatient with Ellen or anyone else trying to come out,
however, I simply think back to my own coming out.
My closet was huge, had a foyer, a turnstile, a few locks,
dead bolts, a burglar alarm with code that all had to be
deactivated, decoded before I could even go for the
door handle. And then there was a storm door. My televised coming out would have been a Ken Burns, ninety-
two-part series. Talk about clithangers.

It wasn't until I had lived with a woman for a year
that it even occurred to me to ask, "Do you think we are
lesbians?" Shortly after that realization, that coming
out to myself, my younger brother stopped by unan-
nounced. It was my partner's and my one-year anniversary and we were upstairs celebrating when I heard my
brother in the downstairs hallway, "Kath? Kath? Are

you all right?" I yelled down to him, "I'm fine. I'll be right down."

As I walked down the stairs, flushed, heart pounding, shoes in hand, I thought, "Well, this is it. Lie or tell him the truth." When he asked again if I was all right, some ghost of lesbians past helped me say, "Jim, I'm really, really fine. We were making love." He'd never heard such sounds except perhaps on video, so he was quite intrigued. We talked the rest of the afternoon. When he had more questions, he was to call and I was to tell the rest of the family.

Coming out causes the most irrational reactions in people, especially family. It is a scientific fact. Perfectly normal people have been known to hold twelve-gauge shotguns to their beloved children's heads upon getting the news. When he got upset later that night, Jim called our oldest brother, Jack, and came out for me. When we met for a coming out luncheon, Jack already knew, and was prepared. A long invisible, yellow, legal pad lay in front of him. On it, a point by point argument against being gay.

Until someone you love blindsides you with the "love the sinner, hate the sin" rationale, you haven't lived. Especially if the sinner in question is you and your life happens to be the sin. When, in summation, my brother—who had been in an all-boys' high school for four years, the seminary for eight years, the army for three years, and then law school for three years—

concluded that it wasn't natural to be with members of one's own sex, I almost spit out my soup du jour. When he finally met and fell in love with his wife, I had been thrilled for him and mistakenly expected the same from him. His final argument was the classic "Don't tell Dad, it could kill him."

The "don't tell Dad" tactic is a weak argument for gays in families, but a strong argument for gays in the military. Think of the money that could have been saved in the Persian Gulf War. One big multipocketed lesbian proclaiming, "I'm a lesbian!" from the top of a sand dune and whole platoons of Iraqis would have bit the dust. Not a shot fired. No property destroyed. The Neutron Lesbian strikes again. Dr. Kevorkian is said to be looking into it.

My brother Bill Clinton jumped across the table in a restaurant when I came out to him, hugged me, and said, "Oh, I'm so glad you're getting some!" I had a feeling he wouldn't have minded watching. Might be the name.

My sister, a physical education major at a state school in upstate New York, said her friends told her I was gay. It was one of the topics of their group house dinner conversations—"Is Mary's sister gay? Discuss." I reminded her that she used to call me a big fat queer. She said she would try it in other areas and since then has called me a big fat millionaire.

It took more time to come out to my parents. Instead

of worrying my security-minded parents that I'd left teaching to perform stand-up comedy, I told them I was giving lectures on women and humor. But the night before leaving on a three-month road trip, I decided to come out to them. As a comedian.

They were getting up to clear the table after dinner, when I said, "Mom, Dad, please sit down, there's something I have to tell you." They both sat down warily. "I'm a . . . comedian." They looked frightened in the pause before "comedian." They looked relieved after "comedian." Their fear, then relief, confirmed my fears that "mass murderer" would have been preferable to their suspicion. It set me back a few more years and I regret involving my brothers and sister in an awkward conspiracy of silence.

Unfortunately, by the time I was confident enough to tell my mother, she was unable to talk because of Parkinson's disease. In one of our last conversations, she told me with great effort that she hoped I would not resent her for not making me get married. I thanked her for not pressuring me. She also told me sadly that I would probably go to hell for not going to church anymore. I asked what kind of god would put me in hell? We would have had a few knock-down-drag-out fights about my being gay, had I told her. I didn't think it was fair to tell her when she couldn't talk back.

My mother had always represented my father as a

strict authoritarian, but he is quite a libertarian and the only thing he has ever been concerned about is my safety and happiness. It did not kill him when I told him I was gay. Not at all. It has enlivened our relationship. One pointer: don't come out to your dad in a moving vehicle.

If my family were larger, I don't think I could have taken such time with each one. I would have made a group announcement or left phone messages: Jack, it's no lack. Bill, it's a thrill. Jim, it's not a him. Mary, it's not scary. Dad, it's not a lad. Mom, sorry for the bomb.

A few years after working through my immediate family, I decided to come out to my nieces and nephews. *Coming Out: The Next Generation.* I suggested to my sibs that I could tell the kids or they could tell them and then we'd talk. My brother Bill opted to tell his two kids first and then have me talk with them. One night over dinner, he told them that their Aunt Kate is a lesbian. His daughter, Angela, then eleven and totally clued, looked disgusted. She valley-girled, "Well duh, Dad. I have only known this my entire life."

Before coming out to my family, I would dedyke my apartment. Some call it "straightening up." Go through bookshelves and take out all the books with "gay" or "lesbian" in the title and put them in backward. It's like being on the wrong side of a trick bookshelf. Look at the pictures on the wall with new eyes, squinting, head tilting side to side. Iris? Labia? Iris? Labia? Go into the fake bedroom and try to make it look like someone has been in there in the last year.

After I came out to my family, there was a period of awkwardness, or shunning, when they didn't visit as much. It is understandable and when I think back on those times, I kind of liked it. I had more time. Now they come to visit. And they like to stay.

Now, instead of dedyking, I crank it up. Leave magazines open in the living room, bathroom. "Gee, Dad, I don't know how flexible you'd have to be to do that with your legs. She *is* clean." Leave huge vibrators out by the bed. "Go ahead, Bill, it's a ten-speed variable, Black and Decker." Or a leather harness on a track over the bed. "Yep, Jim, I rigged it up myself. Watch, it all operates on this little electric box, right here. I can make it go in and pick Mary right out of her chair. Make her hang there like a sister piñata."

An awkward lurch forward and two steps backward has been my process of coming out. For years I told no one. Then I told everyone. Now my approach is more balanced. I like to do subliminal work, especially at delis. "I'll have a half pound of the lesbian Swiss cheese." Or on a plane, in response to the person who asks, "What are you reading?" I'll reply "*This Dyke's Life*—want to see it?" This revelation, judiciously used, can make for more room in coach.

Even though many of my friends espouse outing, I

oppose it. It's punitive, invasive, often vengeful and goes against my prochoice heart. That is not to say that I don't often look the other way when it happens. The person who doesn't want to come out usually should be left inned. If dragged out, we should have the option of saying, "Sorry, we really don't want that one, can we throw him back?"

While I am opposed to outing, I do advocate coming out. National Coming Out Day has grown on me. The first NCOD was in 1988, to commemorate the 1987 March on Washington and on that day, October 11, gay people are encouraged to take their next step in coming out.

The day begs for further development. It already has its imitators—"National Coming Out for Someone Else Day," "National Coming Out with a Vengeance Day," or my favorite, "National Coming Onto Day."

After almost ten years of National Coming Out Day, I am running out of opportunities. I do come out to my oldest brother every year. This does not add to my totals or help me earn the toaster oven, but it *is* good practice. Each October 11 I call him and tell him I'm a lesbian and then we never talk about it again for the rest of the year. And every year when I tell him, he says, "Is that all you can talk about?"

In these last jaded years of the gay nineties, when terminal lesbian chic makes the process of coming out hopelessly outré, coming out is now more important than ever. In Oregon and Colorado, the first states to fight antigay initiatives, state organizers repeatedly stated that when gay people came out and became known to their neighbors, coworkers, church members it became more difficult for straight people to vote against them. In rural areas especially, one can get a false sense of security because of the big triangles on the backs of large farm equipment. One could think, "Ah, slow-moving gay people, I like it here."

But rural gay people have fought off complacency and come out. Their stories are the stuff of local legend and very deep dish. One wonderful story concerns a flight out of Portland, Oregon, one of the antihate states where there had been statewide organizing and raising of political consciousness, savvy, and money.

The flight out of Portland was overbooked, so there was a call for volunteers to get bumped in exchange for free tickets. One man reported to the desk to volunteer. He told the gate attendant that his last name was Gay. She wrote it down and told him to get on the plane, assuring him he would be called if he was needed.

On the plane, there was someone in the man's assigned seat, so he took an open seat. The plane was, in fact, oversold, so the gate attendant sent a flight attendant to find him. She went to his assigned seat and said to the passenger, "Are you Gay?"

The passenger looked up from his reading, flustered, "Excuse me?"

She repeated, "Are you Gay?"

He hesitated, breathed in, and exhaled a devastating paraphrase of Melissa Etheridge, "Yes, I am."

She said, "Well, you've got to get off the plane."

Again, "Excuse me?"

"If you're Gay, you've got to get off the plane."

The real Mr. Gay, realizing the mistake, went up to the attendant and said, "No, *I'm* Gay."

"Well, then *you've* got to get off the plane."

At which point, one very large Jessye Norman queen, two rows back, stood up and said regally, "Well, I'm gay too, and you cannot *force* me from this plane."

alloKate

1. v. to check box on ballot for campaign contribution.
2. fam. Australian greeting.

Potty training in my less-than-direct family involved the exhortation to "do big things for ____" (fill in the blank with the name of a family member or TV personality). As if Dale Evans were going to come walking into our bathroom in one of her big, fringed skirts with her kerchief knotted perfectly around her neck, singing "Happy Trails to You," to admire what you'd done.

That's all I could think about when President Bill Clinton intoned portentously at his Second Inaugural, "Big things don't come from being small." I winced, not because the sentence was such a thudding case in point, but because he had the nerve to pause for applause. And then, I felt bad for Donna Shalala.

Bridge? David Brinkley was right. With speeches like that, you don't think, "Next stop: greatness." You think, "Next stop: boredom." On the oratorical scale from one to Barbara Jordan, it was a three.

One big thing that could come from the little guy is campaign finance reform. Both Bed-and-Breakfast Bill and the Nutty Professor Newt are proof that it's needed. It seems that someone who has run his last race, had his last piece of rubber chicken, stumped his last speech is just the duck to do it. The day after the Inaugs, President Clinton went after soft money. Talk about lame ducking.

Not just money but the length of campaigns must be limited. And I know just how to do it. First we throw a whole bag of chips into everybody's TVs. The technology is there. If I can call in to *ET*, to vote whether or not Liz Taylor should lose weight, I think I should be able to vote for president and other elected officials through my TV.

Campaigns take place only in the final six weeks of the football season. Debates are at halftime. If you don't watch the debate, you don't see the rest of the game. Postdebate analysis is done by John Madden, Bob Costas, and Wolf Blitzer. Citizens vote with their TV remote, "the Remoter Voter," at halftime of the Super Bowl. The new president is announced after the game.

The other half of the population, not at all interested in football, can vote between the garden and garnishing segments on the *Martha Stewart Living* show.

Then we bundle the money we save on the campaigns

and pay off our UN debt, after assuring Jesse Helms, the original bastard out of North Carolina, that certain criteria will be met: the UN headquarters will move to Raleigh, North Carolina, or Mars, and UNC will have first dibs on all really tall basketball players. Madeleine Albright has had a makeover and she is ready to go. Secretary of State, Bill Cohen, is ready to put the gee! back in geopolitical. Just in time.

Shortened campaigns will make primaries and conventions and Dick Morris obsolete, and it will also be a living hell for political comics who've had an easy time of it with longer campaigns and nutbuckets like B-1 Bob Dornan and Ross "Party of One" Perot. But we will sacrifice. We'll do longer investigative pieces about school asbestos removal or the structure of urban governance. It'll be tough, but heck, we'll do it because we want to do big things for our country.

altarKate

---

1. v. to hit a stained glass ceiling.

Singers get away with stuff a comedian could never get away with. We never get to dedicate jokes. We never get to say, "This next series of one-liners I dedicate to my aunt Sophie. I wish she were here tonight. Want to hear? Here's how it goes."

We never get to tell where we got the inspiration for a joke. "This next joke I'd like to do for you tonight, I wrote just after I'd seen my first breaching whale. I was on a trip to Alaska with my father . . . et cetera, et cetera, et cetera," all the way back to a history of water.

We never get to divide up the audience. "The folks on the left will do the setup of the joke. Folks on the right will do the punch line. Then in Spanish, okay? Let's try it." Comics are not good audience members. During sing-alongs, they generally sit pouting, "Hey, darling, I paid twenty-two bucks to get in here, why don't *you* sing a few bars and maybe I'll join in." A comic can ruin a good hootenanny.

Singers get to have backup bands, a dream of mine. If I wrote the songs that make the whole world sing, instead of the jokes that make some of them laugh, I would have a backup band, "Kate and the ClinTones."

Divine inspiration struck one night during a show at an all-girls' Catholic high school in St. Paul, Minnesota. First I asked for volunteers, preferably lesbian ex-nuns. They were there. I'd already sussed it out. Calves are the giveaway. Since the sisters do a modified nun Nautilus kneeling motion every day, with repetitions, they develop distinctive calf musculature. They are cut for Christ.

Three women came up on stage, after I'd singled them out. Two of them, Janie Torie and Janie Toquay, had been in the same convent together and had not seen each other since they left. After a tearful, shrieking reunion, comments about God's will, and some hugs, they answered a few basic questions designed to weed out any backup wannabes.

The questions were basic: When you buy a pagan baby, do you buy it by the pound? Gregorian chant notes, are they round or square? The final question was musical. Is "Eat his body, drink his blood, and we'll sing a song of love" an actual Catholic song or the national S/M anthem? (It's both.)

They aced the questions and became my backup band, the Vessels of Sin. We did a litany, a Caucasian version of call and response, but with a slight twist. In the traditional self-flagellating form, the priest chants, "O, We are a really sinful people," and the congregation responds, "Yes we are."

The Vessels were totally coachable and sang their response in a perfect heartfelt monotone. They posed themselves, hands prayerful, chest-high, eyes heavenward.

KATE: When we say men, we mean women too.

THE VESSELS OF SIN: You gotta be kidding.

K: Adam gave birth to Eve.

VOS: You gotta be kidding.

K: Your lips tell me no dear but there's yes yes in your eyes.

VOS: You gotta be kidding.

K: I promise I won't come in your mouth.

VOS: You gotta be kidding.

K: It's not natural for you two girls to spend so much time together.

VOS: You gotta be kidding.

auntieKate

1. v. to rile up small children before their
   bedtime and then leave.

Family used to be a nice little noun, e.g., "Look, honey,
it's the nuclear family, and why, they're burned to a
crisp," but in the mid-1970s it became an indiscrimi-
nately used adjective. The "family restaurant," the
"family foodstore," the "family movie," the "family fun
place to be." The word "family" described values and
hamburgers with an uncanny leveling effect.

After fifteen years of incessant talk about the family
this, the family that, lesbians and gay men wanted to
have families of their own. The lesbian and gay baby
boom bloomed. The constant drumbeat to return to
family values fused with the disco beat of the gay anthem, "We Are Fam-a-lee."

I have no kids that I am aware of; I love kids so
much I knew not to have them. For me, children, like

cats, suck all the oxygen out of a room. I glaze over and wave after wave of teary-eyed, wide-mouthed yawns begin.

After a near baby-sitting tragedy involving Lincoln Logs and a butane lighter, I knew that it would not be healthy for me to have kids. Certainly not for the kids. Something hideous was bound to happen to my child— she'd fall down in the well, he'd swallow a hammer, drown in the pool—and then I would be devastated for the rest of my life and get shrill and brittle like Mary Tyler Moore in *Ordinary People*.

The gay baby boom came along just in time. I had plumb run out of little nieces and nephews and quite frankly I needed the material. Over the years, my sister, Mary, has been so generous with her kids' comments, I put her on my payroll.

Mary is a great mom; I'm so proud of her. Driving along with her son, five, and daughter, two, strapped in their car seats, they were rocking out with Raffi singing about being happy and gay, when Paul yelled, "Mom, what's gay?" Mary, bopping along, yelled over her shoulder, "Really, really happy." She drove on but had one of her patented "ooojeeze realizations" that maybe he meant more.

At home, he asked again, "What does gay really mean?" Mary took a deep breath. She says motherhood involves lots of deep breathing. She stalled him with a question, "Where did you hear it used?" perhaps hoping the conversation would veer off in a whole word versus phonics discussion. "On the bus. And it wasn't good." They live outside Washington, D.C., and the kids on the bus often use "politician" to insult each other.

She breathed in deeply again. "Well, Paul, when a man and woman get together (Clintonics for "have sex"), it's one thing. But when a man and a man or a woman and a woman get together, that's gay." "Oh, you mean like Urvashi?" he said, naming my girlfriend, not me, already caught in the family conspiracy not to make sexual references to anyone living or dead in his family.

Grace had her own definition of gay. One day while Grace was playing in the basement with a friend, Mary heard her exult, "Let's pretend we're gay!" Mary, at the top of the stairs, neck craned, ear cocked for strains of Johnny Mathis's, "Chances Are," heard Grace's friend ask, "What's gay?" No hesitation, "It's when two girls get together, dance, and have fun."

This graceful logic cannot be dismissed with a Linkletterish kids say the darnedest things. Grace can shift a dominant paradigm. After watching the 1993 March on Washington, she turned to my sister and said, "Now tell me again, Mom, why do ungay people not like Aunt Kate?"

My gaydar has always been on readiness to detect any signs in my nieces and nephews. Paul has moved the needle to full purple alert a few times. When Mary brought Grace home from the hospital, Paul was fine with her, but after a few months, when it didn't look like she was going to be leaving any time soon, he gave her a pop to the head. Mary saw him do it and reprimanded him. She told him he was supposed to protect his sister, not hit her, then asked why he had hit her. He said, "I didn't like her outfit."

When he was three he looked me right in the eye and said, "I still want to grow up to be a girl you know. I like red, but I really like to wear gold." I cut up an old gold lamé coat for his birthday. Another clue came when he announced he wanted to grow up and know everything. He told Mary he wanted to grow up and buy a town house. He didn't say apartment, or mention track lighting, but he did stress town house.

In one after-dinner conversation about children and families, he announced he wanted to grow up to be gay. Mary, who'd had her kids the old-fashioned way, remarked, after a deep breath, "Paul that is certainly an option, but if you do that, you won't be able to have any children." Without missing a beat he said, "Oh, yes I will. I'll adopt. Or I'll take Grace's leftovers." Then he looked at me, but asked his mom, "Can two girls have a baby?" Another breath. "Paul, we have gone over this again and again. A man and a woman can have a baby, not two women." He said, "But they can try, right?"

Lots of gay people are trying and we really don't have the language for it, yet. Not for lack of talking. Everyone's talking about having kids. Over dinner, friends debate fresh sperm versus frozen sperm. And that's just the appetizer.

One friend declined a dinner invitation with "I can't. I have to go upstate to inseminate." Whatever happened to barbecuing?

At one barbecue, I was grilling away, talking to a friend's seven-year-old son, and asked him, "You want a hot dog?" He looked horrified at me and said, "I can't! I'm a lesbian."

Another friend, whose child care fell through at the last minute, had to bring her daughter to a graduate school class she was taking. The baby started to gurgle and coo and try her first word "d . . . d . . . d . . ." and a woman sitting next to her smiled benignly, leaned in and said, "I think she's trying to say Donor."

Gay couples and single parents are trying all manner and methods of child getting—from the old-fashioned way to the simple turkey baster technique, to the more complex procedures, to hiring surrogates, to adoption. Like many straight people, there are gay people who should not have children. One seventy-two-year-old friend confided that she was thinking of becoming a single mother. When she wasn't looking, I stuck a cabbage patch on her arm. The stroller contingents in gay pride parades are larger than the S/M contingent.

Instead of baby showers, we throw going-away parties. Bye! See you in ten years! We had a baby shower for a friend who adopted the sweetest baby boy. I got them a Michelin tire.

The gay baby boom shows some lessening of gay and lesbian self-loathing, or to paraphrase that old Paul Anka song, "I'm having my baby, what a wonderful way of saying how much I love me." But when I ask my friends if they are going to raise their children to be gay, even the most militant of mommas and poppas goes all squishy and dreamy, "She'll be whatever she'll be." Since we are living in one big heterosexual mall, kids need a little extra help to be gay. Oshkosh, tool belts, and trains for the girls. Lamé starter Fiesta ware and Spice Girl accessories for the boys. That's where aunts come in.

antiKwate

1. v. to get older and bolder (var. antiquate).
2. n. a BOBOLINK—Big Older Babe on Lesbian Income, No Kids.

Some mornings I wake up and all I want to do is smoke cigarettes and spit at little boys. It's nothing to be proud of. I am proud that I have quit smoking. Lots of times. Quitting is the hardest thing. They should just call cigarettes "Mom" and get it over with. The patch is very effective for some people; I didn't try it. Other bad behaviors can be treated effectively with patches. A party patch for falling for the most unavailable person in the room. A retail patch. A cocoa patch to avoid all chocolate products.

A huge Joe Camel billboard helped. The sight of that giant scrotum-looking camel with the cigarette hanging from its lips was a visual incentive to quit.

When I tell close friends I have quit, they say they didn't know I smoked. My smoking was so stealthy, so professional, so Marlboro without the scenery that random people felt an unnatural urge to light up.

When I quit it helped to tell myself that I could start smoking again when I'm eighty. I creatively visualized myself on the front porch of some lesbian retirement home, smoking cigarettes and waving at the young girls. I'd be an old toothless babe, hungry for the taste of a little lesbian tartare. Point of information: lesbian retirement homes are not where you go if you want to retire from being a lesbian. That's the suburbs.

The megatrend of baby boomers turning geezer boomers is not lost on entrepreneurial lesbians. Lesbian motor home parks—"Lesbo Rest," "Amazon Manor"—are springing up throughout the south. In Florida and in New Mexico, hundreds of lesbians have circled up the silver bullet–shaped Airstreams, all jacked up on blocks. Blue-and-white scalloped awnings. Multicolored strings of owl lights. Aluminum picnic tables that fold into a briefcase. Green AstroTurf carpet rolled out just so. Bumper sticker: If this van's rocking, don't you come knocking.

Many retirement motor home parks are, I suspect, training sites for secret societies of older women, banding together to take over the world. I hope they are. No one suspects or even notices anything, and yet in planned communities throughout the sunbelt, older women are massing.

They are strictly and hierarchically organized. The

bluer the hair, the higher the rank. Their eyewear offers many clues. The very angle of the clip-on sunglasses—fully raised in permanent surprise or at a glowering perpendicular—speaks volumes to those in the know. Wraparound sunglasses worn over the regular glasses give the impression that the wearer is ready for spot welding at any moment. The women practice flying in formation on oversized three-wheeler bikes with tri-cornered flags snapping in the breeze off large carrier baskets. Elaborate secret codes are embedded in needlepoint. Crocheted multicolored tea cozies are encoded with elaborate plans to take over the computers at Disney World and then commandeer the World Bank.

They are known by their bangs. Older women in bangs melt me. Mamie Eisenhower curlicues lovingly spaced just so, perched high on a large forehead under velveteen pillbox hats. Hint of veil. One wonders how different the Eisenhower years would have been if there had been mousse. It is pure mortification when June Allyson, in her bouncing and behaving bangs, must do Pampers, or Grampers, ads. She might just as well be saying, "Hi. I'm June Allyson and I'm peeing right now."

After a show in San Francisco, I received a letter from my heroes Del Martin and Phyllis Lyon. Together since 1950, they had written an early juicy memoir, *Lesbian/Woman*, long before lesbians were chic. In 1953, they founded the Daughters of Bilitis, the DOB, our DAR. They wrote to say that although they had a good time at a show, they found some of my material disappointingly ageist. Since they are the wind beneath my flannel, lesbos before lesbos were cool, I called them right up.

Del answered the phone in their Bay Area home and got Phyllis on the upstairs line. I told them that I had received their letter, felt terrible about offending them in any way, and had my routine open in front of me. I was ready to go over whatever they found offensive. They thanked me for calling and we started going through the routine.

"Was it the thing about carbon-dating and being older?"

Pause. Silence, then, "No, that's funny. I don't remember you doing that."

"Was it the thing about noticing the chin hair on a friend and not even being able to hear what she is talking about because I am watching the hair, big as a piece of hemp, bobbing up and down, and thinking about yanking it out? Was it that part?"

Pause. Silence. "Hmm. I don't remember that part, do you Del?"

"Having to travel with tweezers for emergency yanking?"

"No, Phyllis, I don't."

To myself, I'm thinking "Oh, please, soon, let someone start laughing. And let it not be me."

But like the nails, I press on.

"Was it the thing about June Allyson? That was probably it."

Silence. "You did something about June Allyson?"

"What was that about?"

"About how there are no roles for older women and how I hate that June's career is reduced to that commercial she does for Grampers. How she might as well say, 'Hi. I'm June Allyson and I'm peeing right now.'"

And mercifully, finally, someone started to laugh.

Phyllis said, "Maybe we got the wrong lesbian comic."

After the call, I did not light up.

authentiKate

1. yer garden-variety lezbin.
2. opp. she wouldn't say lesbian if her mouth was full of one.

The first time I saw *The M-M-M* Reader* in a bookstore, I turned away, afraid someone had seen me see it. My heart started pounding. My ears got red. I had to go to the Self-Help section to calm down.

It was during the Stealth Lesbian Period of Homohistory. If you drew a timeline from the early low-flying, undetected, Stealth Lesbian Period to the flamgirlantly visible Lipstick Lesbian Period, it wouldn't be a straight line. Heck, it wouldn't even be a line. The development of lesbian visibility has nothing to do with geometry and everything to do with quantum physics.

Think of it as a variant on that New Age allegory, "The Hundredth Monkey," a parable about the collective

*m-m-m-aka "lesbian" in the High Stealth Lesbian Period

unconscious. As the story goes, primitive monkeys living on two separate islands had, for thousands of years, suffered death and disease from lack of proper sanitation and no refrigeration.

One day, after years of trial and error, one of the monkeys, the ninety-ninth monkey, went down to the water's edge and washed off her food before eating. The other monkeys watched, screeched, and laughed at her, just before they keeled over from food poisoning. That ninety-ninth monkey did not get sick.

On the neighboring island, monkeys were having the same problem with disease, even though their employees were washing their paws after using the restrooms, and most monkeys were complying with the hair net rules when working the steam tables. Oh sure there was complaining. But one day, without any communication from the ninety-ninth monkey on the other island, another monkey took it into her head to go down to the water's edge and wash off her papaya before eating it. When she didn't get sick, the rest of the monkeys started doing the same thing. Before long they were pooling their tips and putting their savings in mutual funds, but that's another story.

Maybe it was not a New Age parable, but something I saw on the Discovery Channel. Nonetheless, it does illustrate the point. After years of flying, of humming below the radar, Stealth Lesbians emerged in one big Gay bang. Their Lipstick made them visible. Or perhaps it was the cumulative effect of twenty-five years of organizing, protesting, processing, lobbying, phoning, fighting, and coming out.

The lesbian pictured on the cover of *Newsweek* with her girlfriend might actually be Lesbian #100 and #101. Even though I had been out for years and even though I was all alone at my post office box when I first saw *Newsweek*'s cover, I nearly swooned. I looked away, afraid someone had seen me see it. I should have been more used to mainstream depictions of lesbians, but I was not.

After all, k.d. lang had graced the cover of *Vanity Fair* in a risqué shaving scene with Cindy Crawford. There was k.d. butched out, with shaving cream on her face, reclining, waiting for the follicular ministrations of the leggy supermodel. The picture made me want to come back as a razor. For days after, I went around crooning, "Constant Shaving." But the campy photo layout was less shocking than the remarks Jesse Helms, that impotent windsock, made when opposing the nomination of Roberta Achtenberg's appointment to Assistant Secretary of Housing and Urban Development. He described her as "yer garden-variety lezbin."

Newsweek had done a story "Is This Child Gay?" but the cover picture of a Gerber cherub wasn't as direct as Lesbian #100's breathtaking full frontal smile. As a matter of fact, in the earlier gay feature story, of the thirteen pictures of gay people in the article, there was only one picture of a lesbian. And for some bizarre reason, she was lying resplendent, smiling, on a bed. With a pig.

At first I thought the porcine pic was an ink splotch, a smudge, some piece of schmutz, but when I looked more closely, there it was, one of those designer pigs. Of all the pictures of lesbians in the world, why was this one in the article? Did the people from *Newsweek* call her and say, "We're doing an article about gay people, we'd like to come down there, take a picture of you." What did she say? "Come on down. I've got a pig"?

The picture threw off dialogue in my family for a number of months. My eightysomething dad gets *Newsweek* and I knew he'd read the article to learn more about his lesbian daughter. He'd get to the page with the lesbian and the pig and call. I wouldn't be home, so he'd be forced to use my answering machine, which he hates. "Kath? This is your dad." Then he'd leave his number, the same number he's had for forty-three years, because my message said to leave your number. And then, "Do you have a pig?"

But it wasn't just magazines that were covering gays. Television was doing it too. After years of coyness on TV—Paul Lynde, the least square of the *Hollywood Squares*; Lily Tomlin in her purple majesty; the kiss on *LA Law*—television got more to the point. Lynn "I'm So" Sherr did a *20/20* segment on the lesbians of

Northampton, Massachusetts, causing a national lesbian land-rush, "Pull up the stakes, Patience, we're moving back east."

Maria Shriver hosted an hour-long special, *The Gay Nineties*, an examination of the lives of lesbians and gay men at work, at home, in the city, in the country, everywhere. It was evenhanded except for a few bizarre moments. Maria spent some time with a lesbian couple looking through their wedding album, chirping mysteriously, "Oh! we've got a picture like that in our wedding album!" She does?

When she furrowed her brow, tilted her head à la Barbara Walters, and asked, "Did people think it was 'unnatural' for you two to get married?" she double pumped her index fingers to put quotes around "unnatural." "Unnatural." Gay people watching all over America flashed on Maria under Arnold. That's natural?

It was an amazing turn of events, this media-made, so-called Gay Moment or Ho-Moment, although I prefer to think of it as Gay Momentum. And it was almost over before it started. Before Peggy Lee could sing "Is That All There Is?" our fifteen minutes were up and we were in a postgay sixteenth minute. At the very peak of the Gay Moment, the Guttmacher Institute released a study disputing Kinsey's claim that 10 percent of the population was gay. The Guttmacher survey concluded from their numbers that it was more likely that only 1 percent of the population was gay. On closer examination of their methods, it appeared that what the Guttmacher study actually found was that only 1 percent of gay men are *comfortable* saying they are gay. To German people.

While pollsters in the social sciences were trying to find the authentic homosexual, other researchers were looking for a gay gene. They were ignoring the fact that naughty by nature or naughty by nurture was still naughty to a lot of people, and illegal in many states.

One scientist, a gay man, Dr. Simon LeVay, claimed to have found that the hypothalamus was a gland, not a Dr. Seuss character, and also that the hypothalamus of straight men is two times larger than that of gay men or straight women. To my way of thinking, his finding proves two things and neither is that you will know the homo by his hypo: one, scientists are size queens; two, straight men are abnormal.

This hypothalamal information has dangerous consequences. There are antigay people, already in their labs, whipping up big vats of a fast-acting liquid called "Hypo-Grow." They'll put it in spray bottles and then they'll lurk outside gay bars, spraying the smaller unprotected hypothalamal areas on the backs of gay men's necks as they leave the bar. "Got him, Muriel! He'll be straight in a couple of minutes."

Like many other scientists, LeVay did not study lesbians. He explained, without apparent hint of irony, that he was unable to locate any lesbian brains. I've been to that bar too. The only extant study of lesbians concluded all identical twins are lesbian. This was confusing but did explain my unnatural fondness for Hayley Mills. And why Patty Duke could poke a gravy hole in my mashed potatoes any day.

Despite all this scientific attention on gays, I wasn't enjoying this newfound scrutiny. I'm not antiscience—my passion for microwave popcorn supports that—but I hate all the genetic studies. So what if a gene or a gland causes gayness? Would that make the coming-out-to-parents conversation a health report? "Mom, Dad, I've got the gay gene." Would protest signs that say "We're here, we're queer, get used to it" become apologies—"We've got the gay gene, we couldn't be more sorry" or "I wish my hypothalamus were bigger"?

The gay liberation movement was explained away by endocrinologists and behaviorists and the media dubbed the lesbian liberation movement "Lesbian Chic." For months producers on talk shows all over the country yelled to their assistants, "Get me that short lesbian!" "Now, get me that blond lesbian!" "No, no, no. Get me that lesbian that reads." Lesbianism was reduced to a fashion statement.

The Lesbian Avengers fought the market's good-girlieization of lesbians' lives by organizing fierce Dyke Marches. Thousands of lesbians marched chanting, "We're dykes, don't touch us, we'll hurt you!" a chant which at first frightened me, but which I have since used to get service at Lumber Superstores.

Scientists and gay apologists did too good a job convincing America that lesbians are genetically condemned to a life of long laps in the well of loneliness. Such a good job that when Ann Heche announced on *Oprah* that she was not gay but had seen Ellen DeGeneres "across a crowded room" and had just fallen in love, everyone, but Ellen, was confused. The use of the phrase "across a crowded room" upset a lot of gay people who felt the phrase should only be used in *South Pacific* by Ezio Pinza lest Ann veer off into "Happy Talk Keep Talking" with snappy hand gestures. Oprah put on her best confused face and had to schedule a special emergency show about the origins of gayness. During sweeps week.

After two or three bible-humping audience fulminators ran unchecked about abomination, Oprah said the show was a nonjudgmental, value-free attempt to understand the origins of homosexuality. To understand Ann and Ellen, Oprah brought in several experts, including three men who only studied other men but were as comfortable with the topic of women's behavior as priests are discussing marriage.

The women panelists, except for Judy Wieder, editor of *The Advocate*, seemed to have been chosen for their inarticulateness. One woman panelist tried to describe how the same thing that happened to Ann had happened to her—she'd been married twice and then, blammo, she'd fallen in love with a woman. JoAnn

Loulan, career lesbian and author of the very brief book *Lesbian Sex*, announced in a helium-induced shriek that although she identified as a lesbian, she had a boyfriend. How could that be? Wasn't that an old Polish joke?

Loulan observed that often straight women have their most intimate friendships with other straight women and then added dangerously that it was too bad that they didn't act on the sexual feelings they often had for each other. All over America, people scratched their collective heads. Such monkey business. Oprah was up in a flash saying that she had a best friend Gayle and that she never, never, never (they went to commercial, came back and Oprah was still never, never, nevering) ever felt attracted to her friend. Ninety-six negatives make a positive.

But Ellen has nothing on *Xena, Warrior Princess*. The show, a spin-off of *Hercules*, features Xena, a descendent of She-Ra, Princess of Power. She of the crossed wrists was a favorite of mine because if she got a little pissed, rockets would shoot out of her breasts. I would like to see that in the Senate. *"The senator from Utah doesn't agree with that?"* Blam, blam.

The Xena writers made Xena the guardian of Gabrielle, queen of the Amazons and, even more dangerous, a poet. Some of my Xenamaniac friends had taped every episode by the time I found the show mid-surf. My thumb froze. There was Xena buck naked in a steamy bathtub with Gabrielle looking like a young, wet Holly Near. As Xena sponged off the dirt buildup under Gabby's leather bustierre with her medieval loofa mitt, they played twenty questions. If Ellen DeGener-Morgan had put on a leather breastplate in her first episode, cut in some bangs, she could have puffed out her chest and announced, "For I am Ellen of Morgan and I am queen of the lesbians," and no one would have even cared.

The night I went to the Grammy Award ceremonies convinced me that the great unpolled America was cool. In exchange for a number of sexual favors my lawyers have advised me not to go into at this time, Ellen got me tickets to attend the Grammys at Madison Square Garden. I arrived late, it was pouring rain, there were double barricades all around, and the cabdriver let me out on the wrong side of the Garden. I ran up to a policeman.

"You've got to help me get in. I've got tickets."

"Yeah? Where dja get em?"

I hesitated but said, "From Ellen DeGeneres herself."

"Yeah? You her girlfriend?"

"Right. Do you think she'd treat her girlfriend like this? Leaving her out in the rain on the wrong side of the Garden. Does the word limousine mean anything anymore?"

He wasn't even listening. He was calling to his buddy.

"Joey, get ova here. Don't you think she'd like my sister?"

And he starts to fix me up with his sister.

"Thanks but I've got a girlfriend and she's in there and it's our ninth anniversary and if you don't get me in, there won't be a tenth anniversary."

He swung open the barricades, waved me through. "Fuhgeddaboudit."

compuKate

1. v. to throw a computer out the window.
2. not dot calm.
3. phr. out of the chatrooms, into the streets!

At 6:00 P.M., the coffee machine switches on automatically, but since there is no water in it, just a basket of old grounds, it sighs and blows out brown coffee steam. During a very quiet moment in *Secrets and Lies*, my watch alarm starts beeping like a new age fart and two gay men in the audience think it's time to take their meds. After a power outage, every digital appliance in the house flashes on and off. In the darkened bedroom the bed is flanked by lights from the clock radio and the VCR, resembling a secret airfield.

In Los Angeles, I lock myself out on the patio of a friend's all-digital house. I can't get her outside pool phone to work. I don't remember the secret code to deactivate the alarm system. As I try to jimmy the screen, the alarm starts pulsing and felonious-looking security

men in their impressive Ford Escorts roar into the driveway. I can't remember her secret password when they
ask. Under pressure, I cannot remember my ATM number for bail money.

Historically, while I appreciate this century's enfran-
chisement of women, technologically, I feel born into the
wrong century. In a few years, in the new millennium, I'll
be able to feel twice as bad. My own slow-down-you-
move-too-fast generation is responsible for the current
speed of things, but I am more comfortable with my own
bovinity and oppose most emerging technologies. If I
could, I'd vote against beepers, cell phones, fax ma-
chines, zip drives, most VCRs. I would vote in favor of
Eric's Ultimate Solitaire, automatic coffee makers if I get
the A.M./P.M. programmed right, and TV remotes.

While my little friends thought they had a constitu-
tional right to their own individual pink Princess phones,
my family treated phones as if they were some newfangled
space-age contraption featured at the 1939 New York Ex-
position. My grandmother thought phones caused cauli-
flower ears. Or brain worms. My dad still looks at the
earpiece before he puts a phone to his ear. Long-distance
calling from Syracuse to relatives in Buffalo was so exotic,
we waited until 11:00 P.M. when everyone was incoherent
with fatigue but the rates were lower. Each of us asked my
aunt about the weather in Buffalo (snow), then handed
the phone off like a hot potato.

Ma Bell and I have always had a problematic

relationship. I don't like talking to people who aren't there, and I long for the day when all my friends are in the same area code. I resent phones and most phone-related technology. When Ma changed my first phone exchange from the words "Howard eight oh eight one oh!" to numbers, I had my first bout of techno-resentment. Now I resent digital translation, "1-800-BIG-BABE," and find enforced mnemonics annoying. My personal hard disk for phone numbers is either full up or damaged.

My resentment toward phones makes me act out. Phones are unilateral, for me to call you. Just because someone leaves a message on my machine does not mean that I have no choice but to respond. My message never says, "I'll get back to you." Callers who leave long slow messages that are more audition than message, and then slur speedily through their number so you have to play back through the whole damn thing to decode the number, do not deserve a call back. Nor do those who leave "I know you're there. Pick up. Pick up. Pick up—" like some demented parrot.

After a misguided, month-long free trial of call-waiting got me roped into entirely too many auctions and benefits, I became an unapologetic screen queen, a girl who can say no.

Mine is not a violent smashing Ludditism but more a horseless carriage, Andy Rooneyish, grousing techno-distrust and an annoying feeling that I am so no courant. As yet there are no support groups for such retro techno-peasantry. If, however, you use the word "Dot" when you introduce yourself and you're no Dorothy, or friend of Dorothy, chances are you should be in a support group for those addicted to the Internet.

When we were kids, my father was head of EDP, electronic data processing, in charge of the huge room-sized temperamental computer processor that did the monthly power bills. This machine had an uncanny knack for crashing just as my mom jammed the last thing in the beige Ford for a family vacation. Computers have always been associated with nuisance.

About the only thing I have found good about the new technologies is grief management. When my mother died in 1984, I got my first computer. I spent hours trying to maneuver the mouse, create new files, and decipher those spiral computer guidebooks. Mercifully, time passed. One friend bought a VCR when her father died; she mastered it as if she were sitting shivah. She got so good, she is now her community's designated taper.

Every time I'm on a computer, it's woman versus machine; Kate versus Big Blue Mac. I am a nincomputer and have no business being on a computer. Just when I get comfortable, the system becomes obsolete or incompatible with everything else. I would have been happy with my original Macintosh eight-track, but I live with the Emerson Fitipaldi of computer geeks whose mantra is "You need more speed!" I took a computer course at a local community college, which was like attending a high school with ashtrays, and was just starting to think that a computer was more than a typewriter hooked up to a TV screen when she talked me into getting a faster, smaller, portable Macintosh. It looked like a portable sewing machine, weighed about twenty pounds and did not come with Sherpas. The battery was a huge dense hunk of what I imagined the black box is made of.

My third Macintosh is a Powerbook 5300cs. The cs stands for crock of shit. It has crashed three times—screen awash in eerie sepia, no response, kaput compute. I'm on a first-name basis with many of the repair people on the emergency 800 number—when I can get through. Their on-hold time is quite long, but I have grown fond of their classical music selections. Sometimes during interminable Public Radio pledge drives, I put them on speaker phone.

The last time my computer flat-lined I spoke to a lovely man, named Duryea, from East Africa. As I described the problems he listened and typed, clicking away on the work order form. In summation, I told him it was so bad, the computer was leaking lemon juice. I heard him typing that in and tried to stop him. He began to chastise me about beverages near my computer. I explained it was an American saying. "When life gives you lemons, make lemonade" is from East Africa.

For mini-crashes, I go to my local computer repair place, TekServe. Their door chime is the sound of a

Mac booting up. A bright red Coke machine sells ten-cent pony bottles. An old computer terminal has been gutted and houses a very active ant farm. Most of the TekServers are young grunge guys and gals who could just as easily be fixing dirt bikes. When I described what my computer wasn't doing, Deb interrupted and said it sounded like a blown logic board. I felt proud.

Word processing provides a way to cover my pitiful typing skills without gallon drums of Wite-Out or giant eraser holes. In my Catholic high school, there was only one typewriter and that was in the principal's office. Typing class opened with a prayer for typewriters and was more of a discussion group than anything hands on. At some point, Sister Mary Pica would pull down a screen in the front of the room that showed us what a typewriter keyboard would have looked like if the sale of the chocolate ingots had gone better. We were always hawking something for equipment.

My parents thought the class was a waste of time, unlike Religion IV, and sent me to the public summer school for typing. I persuaded my friends to go with me and we pretended it was Summer Typing Camp. Most of us had never even been inside a public school and felt like renegades. We all acted out. We put the gray plastic IBM Selectric covers on our heads and pretended we were the Sisters of the Flying Cap.

Since it was public school, I felt like I could cheat, so I always snuck looks at my fingers. Therefore, I have no confidence in my typing and while I might get all the right letters in a word, most of them are in some reversed order, like old Gaelic. I have never typed "people" correctly, for instance. And if I do get the order correct, I will have typed a capital letter for no reason— e.g., pEople.

Often, especially with E-mail, I type in all caps. But according to rule 1,421.a in the book of International Netiquette, typing in all caps equals yelling. Good thing e. e. cummings is not alive to send eee-mail. His friends would write back, "WHY ARE YOU WHISPERING?" For such a wild and free, supposedly unregulated new frontier as cyberspace, there are many rule kittens.

When the screen freezes and a dialogue box announcing, "A system error, type .01, has occurred" accompanied by an icon of a small black bomb with its fuse lit, the only response is "OK." It's not okay. Options for any cyberian at that moment are computer defenestration or getting stoned.

Unfortunately, my only rule is never work on your computer if you are stoned. It's easy to get lost, have no idea how you got into a chat room, how to get out, or what your password is. Once, I thought I was maneuvering like a hip cybernaut through the World Wide Web, and it turned out I was stalking someone and didn't even know it. Another evening as I was working late on my memoirs, a little message came up on the screen, "You are almost out of memory."

domestiKate

1. v. to get married (var. domastiKate).

It happened when I was reading one of the glossy gay magazines now delivered to my door. Now, *there's* a sentence you didn't used to hear. If any gay magazine was delivered to your door in the past, it wasn't glossy but low-grade newsprint, in a plain brown wrapper. Or it was that ur-zine, the proto-zine out of Michigan, *The Lesbian Connection. LC* was an early networking newsletter for lesbians looking for other lesbians and usually arrived disguised as a Bostitch Staple Ball. Before trying to pry it open, you had to have your tetanus shot updated.

That was then, this is now. Now all manner of gay magazines are delivered bold as brass to the door. Lots of them have Out in the title. *Out and About* for the gay traveler. *Rainbow Trout* for the gay sportfisher. *Doubt*, a

magazine for the bisexual. *Pout*, a magazine for Gay
Republicans.

Actually, I was looking at the high-fashion, high-
gloss pictures in *Ümlout*. Because we've got pictures!
Famous gay people. Famous dead suspected gay people.
Famous live suspected gay people with blurred fists fish-
eyeing toward the camera. Famous gay couples. Famous
gay half sisters with famous political brothers playing
ministers at gay weddings on gay-friendly sitcoms.

Actually, I was looking at the ads. We aren't so
much a movement anymore as a niche market waiting
to be scratched. We've got mountains of thangs to buy.
In between the ad for gay cruises ("The only straights
you'll see are Gibraltar!") and the one for gay colonics
("Swallow a prism, shit a rainbow") I spotted an ad for
"The Freedom to Marry Kit." I wondered, "Who is Kit
and why do we want to marry her?"

The FTM kit is an actual kit designed to help
concerned gays organize in their municipalities for the
freedom to marry. Traditionally, the mere promise of a
decoder ring could spur me into frenzied feats of activity.
But now I'm just waiting for this Gay Cana Mania to
blow over.

Gay couples have always been interested in marry-
ing but it all finally bubbled up in, of all places, the fiftieth
state, Hawaii. Three couples sued for the right to marry.
A gay couple in Ithaca, New York, had also wanted to
sue, but they were dissuaded from pursuing their case by

the Gay C.L.U., who told them that no one wanted to honeymoon in downstate New York. Go to college there, sure, but nobody wanted to do a hula in January in a down vest.

The deep magma of marriage bubbled up to a Diamond Head, and the defense for the plaintiffs, Don Homo and Magnum P.I.G., said they were being discriminated against if they could not get married. The prosecution basically said, "Whatever happened to just getting leied?"

Other states worried that they would have to recognize the Hawaiian unions. So they got together and men who had been married a number of times apiece passed the Defense of Marriage Act (DOMA). Lord knows it needed defending, but not from gay people. If they'd really been serious about defending it, they'd have called in the Bureau of Alcohol, Firearms, and Tobacco.

The day the president signed DOMA, the movie *First Wives Club* opened in theaters and Bette, Goldie, and Diane did a great deal to show that men really meant to sign DORA, the Defense of Remarriage Act.

You don't get to pick your issues in movements, but I would have thought we would have gone for something else. Perhaps violence against gays. Or perhaps welfare reform, which certainly affects people living with AIDS, or the disproportionately high number of lesbians with breast cancer.

But no, the issue du fin de siècle for gays is the freedom to marry. Go figure. Everyone is talking about it. It's Mad Vow Disease. Like balancing the budget, it seems the longed-for panacea—if we can just get married, the millennium can start.

I have applied rigorous self-criticism to understand why this issue does not exactly knock the dots off my dice. It's not the first time I have had to work up enthusiasm for a gay issue. Gays in the military was a challenge to my antimilitary heart. Instead of thinking that I was enthusing about gay guys convincing their dads that they were man enough to kill other men, I got there by thinking of it as a jobs program. Not full steam. Think vaporizer.

Of course I believe that gay people should have the right to marry and have the same benefits accruing to straight married people, but for myself, I prefer living in sin.

One time after discussing my hesitations about this marriage issue, a woman came up to me after my show with a long accordion-pleated green-and-white striped computer printout of the four hundred reasons why gay people could save money if they got married. My personal favorite, and actually the reason I became involved in the gay liberation movement in the first place, was #324. My partner and I could save money on our fishing license. And on our subscription to *Rainbow Trout*.

The freedom not to marry is one of the things I have enjoyed about being gay. So is the freedom not to have children. Because so many gay people are raising children, it follows that they would want the civil protections of marriage for those children. Children have been so well-protected within straight marriages.

Some of my straight friends support gay marriages because they don't see why they have to be the only ones who suffer through painful divorces. Some of my gay friends are getting married just for the things. Many get to a point in their relationship when they look at each other and say, "Honey, we don't have a matching Tupperware top in the whole house, what do you say we get married?"

Don't get me wrong. Anything that gets gay people incensed, involved, interested in the gay movement is wonderful. I'm just having an "Is That All There Is?" Moment.

Instead of spending time on the freedom to marry, I think we should try to talk straight people out of getting married. It's not going well for them. Nicole/O.J. Lisa Marie/Michael. I could go on. This certainly would cut down on a whole range of civil service jobs. See, I'm doing my best to balance the budget.

It's hard to be gay and a people pleaser. This FTM mini-movement seems to be fueled by a desire to show that we can be upstanding citizens, registered for the draft and at Barneys, with children, and that we too will keep sex within the confines of marriage. As if.

What bugs me is that after all is said and done, we get

the word "partner." It sounds so businesslike and is as limited as "lover." If we did it as much as we are accused of doing it, lover would suffice. But partner is so western I expect tumbleweed to dance by. Partner sounds so *The Quick and the Dead*, with Sharon Stone, the woman who made me want to come back as a saddle.

Much like the boy in *A Thousand Clowns* who changed his name until he found one he liked, I've been experimenting with what to call my partner. I haven't tried Chevrolet yet. We've worked our way through consort, inamorata, squeeze, and some confectionary words. So far "ATM" is the favorite.

dupliKate

1. thanks for cloning; wait for the sheep.
2. here's looking at ewe, kid.

On the cusp of Women's History Month, the papers announced that an embryologist from Scotland had for
the first time successfully cloned a sheep whose fleece
was white as snow. He named it Dolly. When asked for
comment on the implications of such a discovery, the
fabulously named Dr. Ursula Goodenough, a cell biolo-
gist at Washington University, quipped, "There'll be no
need for men."

Before examining less promising implications, let's
take a look at the great Scot and what he did. Dr. Ian
Wilmut, Oscar-nominated star of *Babe* and a father of
three children whose names he could not remember, is
described by his colleagues as "careful, diligent, honest,
and thoughtful." That's supposed to make us all feel

better, but somehow it doesn't quite allay my worries. Plus, he wears sheep cologne.

Even though for years gay men have been successfully cloning in San Francisco's Castro District, the day after the announcement and faster than you can say "how to make a knapsack bomb," the instructions for cloning were on the Internet at www.a new ewe. org. I downloaded them and despite the "do not try this at home" warning, I did. Like my attempts to replicate the cold fusion experiments of Pons and Fleischman, which only resulted in mason jars of Constant Comment sun tea all over the kitchen, my efforts failed.

The recipe seemed quite simple: First, take a cell from a sheep and keep it in a tissue while removing the DNA-containing nucleus from an unfertilized sheep's egg. So far, so good. Then fuse them together into an embryo.

As in every great family recipe, Dr. Wilmut left out one crucial ingredient. Try as I might, I could not get them to fuse, even though I played "Peter and the Wolf" very softly in a darkened room. Might have used the wrong voltage. I was, therefore, unable to transfer the embryo into the surrogate mother sheep, as Dr. Wilmut had done, where it was supposed to divide and develop like a normal embryo. It's probably just as well. My apartment is tiny and there are rules about pets.

Culture watchers note the enormous implications of this scientific development:

- Miss Shari Lewis won't have to buy new tube socks.
- With the cry "No pelf from pelts!" the Polar Fleece lobby will fight for criminalization of sheep's clothing.
- Nursery rhymes will have to be updated:
  "Mary had a little lamb, all by herself."
- Children's songs will have to be updated:
  "Old MacDonald had a farm ey I ey I oh
  and on his farm he had . . .
  a pigsheep—with an 'oink bah' here
  and an 'oink bah' there
  a chicken and a four-wheel—with a 'jeep jeep'
  here
  and a 'jeep jeep' there . . ."
- Pope John Paul, who himself has been cloned from a large kielbasa, will summarily excommunicate Dr. Wilmut, even though he is not a Catholic. That "Lamb of God" song will be revised.
- My *Daughter, Myself* will become a best-seller from the Boston Women's Health Book Collective.

Meanwhile, Woolite workers are doing overtime. Insomniacs are thrilled. Condom makers, ecstatic. Narcissists, vindicated. Term limits, obsolete.

Unlike Dr. More Than Goodenough, my first thought

was not the end of husbandry. One of the most trou-
bling implications of sheep cloning is the seeming in-
evitability of human cloning. While medical ethicists
wrangle, perhaps the best argument against human
cloning is Dr. Richard Seed from Ohio who is rushing
to be the first to clone human bipeds. His motivation?
To win the Nobel Prize. He needs the money to get his
house trailer out of hock.

eduKate

1. v. to be as in charge as a referee in professional wrestling.

Even though it has been almost twenty years since I taught high school English, I still get a thrill from snow days. Until recently. What happened to make the thrill begone did, however, help me break a tragic dependence on that New Age fireplace, the Weather Channel, and its amiably frumpy host Joanetta Jones.

The school closing announcements during a three-day blizzard stopped my almost nonstop monitoring of Jones's monitoring of the weather. The announcements crawled in a ticker-taped understatement along the bottom of my screen. I had no idea there were so many private religious schools.

Unlike the hardier public schools, private Christian schools were the first to close:

The New Day Day School, closed.

The All God's Children Got Wings School, closed.

The Homosexuals Must Die Middle School, closed.

The John Doe #2 Brigade School, closed.

The Apocalypse Pretty Soon School, delayed one hour.

The underground tunnel will remain open.

And my favorite: "Mrs. Delbert Coles of Ipswich, Massachusetts, would like to announce to her three children, Sarah, Charlene, and Mark, that her home-schooling classes are canceled for today only."

The intrusion of religion on the secularity of the weather was just too danged much for me. I quit watching.

Lamar Alexander would have loved all those private schools. He'd spent his whole time as Secretary of Education during the Bush administration trying to eliminate the Department of Education. After that, he ran for president, another office he seemed bent on destroying. Now he is the senior model for the J. Crew catalog, the plaid shirt division.

Alexander's attitude and the drive toward private schools barely masks the wholesale bailout on the public school system. What's up with that? That's Ebonics for "Why?" Just as many of us were getting proficient in Esperanto, along comes the Oakland School System and a new teaching fad. I don't care if it's Ebonics or

High Colonics as long as people are talking about education.

As a teacher, I got so sick of sitting alone on Parent Teacher Night that I organized a teachers' pool. Every teacher put in two bucks and whichever two teachers had the least or the most numbers of parents at the end of the night split the pot. At least, I thought, I could make a little money for my wasted time. I won three parents' nights in a row for fewest visitors. It became too easy. So I decided to try to win for the most parent visitors.

Parent Night fell during the annual junior year unit on Macbeth. The pedagogical fashion at the time stressed making things interesting for students, as opposed to earlier times when force-feeding and shock treatments were popular. I tried lots of different methods with my kids, who were what our guidance counselor/junior varsity football coach called "yer terminal students." That meant that high school was the end of the educational line for them. Most of them were bussed long hours to vocational schools where they learned plumbing, welding, secretarial, nursing, and other trades. In one year they would be making more than me, if they weren't out-earning me in their part-time jobs already.

For one of their unit assignments, each student was to create a mobile to illustrate the dramatic structure of Macbeth. Given their trade skills, the MacMobiles were dazzling. We hung them for Parent Night. When I looked through the suspended mobiles, I said to a student sitting directly under one, "Bob, it would be a good idea if you moved your desk quickly to the left."

As he buttwalked his desk to the left, the wire hanger that had been holding the five pound hunting knife directly over Bob's fontanel let go. The knife fell and stuck in the floor. We all watched as the red construction paper blood drops fluttered to the ground. The mobile's creator told me the knife symbolized the climactic moment when Banquo was killed by Macbeth. Better it fell then and not later that night. Open house was a full house.

At the end of that day's classes, I had reminded my students that if they got their parents to come, they would receive extra credit. Then just as a throwaway line, I told them if they could get their parents to recite one of Macbeth's soliloquies, I'd boost their average. Their ears perked up. I was so unused to their attention, it threw me. I continued, "if your parents can recite a soliloquy while tap-dancing, I'll add ten points directly to your average." I was kidding, I swear.

Parent Night started at seven, but I got there early to make sure there had been no more MacMobile Disasters. I opened the door, hit the lights, and heard, "A one and a two and a three . . ." and the mother of one of my failing students entered with a stutter step, reciting, "Is this a dagger I see before me, the handle toward my hand?" The parents lined up in the hallways like a community theater audition for A *Chorus Line*. The teacher I shared the classroom with got so annoyed, I had to pay her off with some of my winnings.

When interviewers ask where I got my comedy training, I tell them teaching high school English. Usually there are no further questions about my credentials. When people ask me incredulously, "How can you do two shows a night?" I tell them that for eight years I did five shows a day. For two years I taught on split sessions. The senior high met in the morning from 7:00 A.M. until noon, then the junior high used the building. I monitored the cafeteria lunch at 10:00 A.M., watching pubescent boys, who played hockey and took their front teeth out to eat, gum squares of school pizza. Talking to a group of girls, cross-eyed from peeling back their split ends, is great training for a tough night of comedy.

Teaching is performance art. During one of the first lawn mowing days of spring, my students were watching the maintenance man ride back and forth, back and forth on the power mower. I was talking to the right side of everyone's faces. No one noticed when I left the room. I went outside, hopped on the mower behind the surprised maintenance man, like Dennis Hopper in *Easy Rider*, and roared by the room, waving.

When I began teaching it was the tail end of the open classroom movement. I designed units in Sports Writing, Humor, and Death. The humor class was deadly; the class on death was often wildly funny. Fridays were game days and I created games that tested students on what we had studied during the week. I was Alice Trebec and got very jaded seniors to compete for multicolored rolls of tart Smarties as if they were sticks of gold.

Within two years of beginning my teaching career, the walls that had come down to create open classrooms were starting to go back up. I was called into the office for a conference with the head of the school board, a right-to-life father of twelve, and was interrogated about my unit on death. He accused me of teaching euthanasia. I began to support retro-abortion. The dreaded, grim "back to basics" movement had begun and grammar became more basic and deadlier than death. After eight years, I wanted out of teaching because of illness and fatigue. I was sick and tired of it.

When I first left teaching, I was surprised to find that there were so many people on the streets during the day. It was all I could do not to ask for a hall pass. Once I almost told an unsuspecting civilian to put out the cigarette. It seemed like we were all outside on one long fire drill. It took me about ten years to begin measuring a year from January to January and not September to June. At the end of every August I still have an unnatural fondness for knee socks and have one or two teacher nightmares involving being tragically underdressed for my first class.

Most of all I miss the students. One day I was going over special spelling rules for single and plural with my students. They hated them. And me. It did seem for every rule there was an exception. They thought I, the spelling sadist, made them up overnight to trick them. I was working with one of my favorite students, Steve Tubolino. "Steve, spell the plural of leaf." He looked at me, paused, gave me that no-problem, can-do look and spelled, "T-R-E-E."

forniKate

1. best with lubriKate.
2. in Clintonics, to get together.

For those of you (especially my straight friend Jon) who turned to this chapter first, thinking, "Irish. Catholic. Lesbian. Won't be a very long chapter," this is a very painful chapter. The lubriKate chapter is sorely missed. At first, the purpose of this chapter was to answer the question "What do lesbians do in bed?" because I happen to know. I've had more lovers than most people have tongues.

But in the nineties, no one even asks what lesbians do in bed because they already know, because they don't care, or perhaps because they don't want to get icked out. The question most asked of lesbians these days is not "What do you do in bed?" but rather "Who's the father?" The etiquette issues surrounding the eternal paternal question are brilliantly answered by Miss

Lesbian Manners in her book *Everything You've Ever Wanted to Know About Gay Sex But Were Too Icked Out to Ask,* in an excellent chapter entitled "The Smoking Schlong."

No matter what lesbians do in bed, or on other surfaces in the home, one of the best features is that so far there is absolutely no way to get pregnant. Quelle relief. Lesbian sex gives new meaning to the term "safe sex" and that's why it's so dangerous.

For the safest sex, lesbians are encouraged to use dental dams. A dental dam is not a cuspid curse, e.g., "A pox on your bicuspids!" but that little 3″ ×5″ piece of latex that dentists use to isolate the area in the mouth that he or she is working on. When they (the dams, not the dentists) are in place during sex, they prevent the exchange of bodily fluids. They are very big in some sections of the country. Big as in popular. Although some women in Iowa have been known to get a big old Hefty trash bag, clip off the corners, step in, pull it up, and cinch it off. One woman from Des Moines uses suspenders with the cinchless store brand.

Dental dams can sometimes cause problems. In Northampton, Massachusetts, where there is both a high density of lesbians and lesbians in dentistry and the winters are long, a dentist was working on a woman, a lesbian. She put the dental dam in place in the woman's mouth, started the drill, and the woman in the chair came in thirty seconds.

A group of hygienists claims to be the first to suggest using dental dams for safe sex. Good thing it wasn't a group of meat packers or foreplay would involve a lot of shrink-wrapping and Saran Wrap.

Since researchers rarely study women, necessity often invents uses for household products in the prevention of motherhood—hangers, vinegar, lunches to pack. The male, ever fascinating to himself, is endlessly, minutely researched. They've got product to prove it. Hundreds of condoms designed with special features, flavors, and sizes.

One morning I turned on breakfast television to see Katie Couric interviewing a lovely looking woman. Chyroned under the woman's head was her name and the words "sex educator." On the table between them, in a sea of shiny mylar squares with the embossed condom circle, standing at attention like some flesh-colored stalagmites, were two dildos. The woman calmly talked pseudo-mystified but dexterous Katie through putting a condom on the dildo. It was 7:37 A.M. Had my coffee been spiked? Despite such advances, a study found that men just don't like to wear them.

The solution to the problem of men not wanting to wear condoms was to make women wear condoms. That made sense to people. The company that developed the condom for women rejected the name "Vagina Dentata" cheekily proposed by some of the boys up in advertising, in favor of the more subtly ironic "Reality." It looks like a bread bag. Not a big Wonder Bread loaf, more a baguette or perhaps half a baguette.

Mercifully, these are not my worries. Never have been. I've never actually done it with a guy. I have been told that this qualifies me for the lesbian Gold Card, with frequent flier miles in Arkansas. It's not that I never met the right guy, as my burly man's man accountant often suggests helpfully, the deeper suggestion being that he's Mr. Right Guy. I've met some fabulously sexy guys. Some of them were even straight. I just never felt I could drink enough.

I'm lucky I ever had *any* sex. Living in a house full of brothers was like living in the House o' Penis. Sex was a male thing, and like the guns of Navarone, those things apparently could go off at any time.

Masturbation was a big problem for my brothers. It was not a problem for me, because no one would tell me what it was or what was involved. I looked it up in an annoyingly vague but strictly imprimatured Catholic dictionary. It said, "masturbation = self abuse." That didn't give me a clue as to what to do or where to start.

Thirty years later, masturbation is still a problem for people. Surgeon General Joycelyn Elders was forced to resign because she spoke about it in a larger discussion about safe sex and pregnancy. People reacted as if she had masturbated with a crucifix in front of thousands of people while singing something about Argentina. The People Against Sex Except for Procreation Auxiliary demanded her resignation. In protest, a friend of mine had "I Masturbate and I Vote" bumper stickers made. That gave a whole new meaning to "pulling the lever."

According to my mother and to Mother Church, the only purpose of sex was to be a mother, and since I knew I was not going to have kids, I resigned myself to the fact that there would be no sex for me. I had early Ethan Frome/Silas Marner damage and knew that I would end up tatting and darning socks in the evening by my older brother's hearth.

The antisex force field of my youth—God, the guardian angel snitch with the Tripp wire on my right, my mother, her spies, the church—was like a sex surveillance system with hidden cameras and heat sensitive sprinklers. Dogs didn't even do it on our block. The force field was in equal and opposite proportion to some undeniable sexual energy that hummed around me and my brothers. When we were little and watched TV together, whenever we spotted a hint of cleavage, we'd nudge each other, do Groucho eyebrows, and hoot "WooWoo!"

My dear mother only talked to me regarding sex twice. First the eroto-cryptic "Sex is dirty; save it for someone you love."

The second time she was in a wheelchair with Parkinson's disease. Mom told me that she'd been watching Phil Donohue and had to get up to turn it off. "But Mom, you can't walk. Remember? What were they talking about?" She said it was a show about sex and "they were talking about orgasms like they were three for a nickel."

All praise to Phil Donohue and Dr. Ruth! And while we're at it praise be Peter Pan, Julie Andrews, and the women's movement. Mary Martin as Peter, no less, gave me hope. My profound physical reaction to Julie Andrews in *The Sound of Music* hinted to me that I did have a few of my own favorite things. The women's movement, despite its expulsion of "the lavender menace," got the dangerous message through to me that I had choices.

And finally one night in a Dodge Colt in Boston's Back Bay after a St. Patrick's Day parade, I chose. Every tutala tutala was where I knew it would be. We jigged until the windows steamed. I became proficient in Gaelic. Unfortunately we were both Irish Catholic, first-born girls and what became a relationship crumbled under the weight of guilt and shame. Thankfully, my next relationship was with a woman who had been raised Quaker and had no concept of guilt. Try as I might.

I wish lesbians did it as much as we are accused of doing it. My personal preferences inexplicably have to do with barometric pressure. A good low leaves me weak. That explains my fascination with the Weather Channel. One summer in Provincetown, as everyone was boarding up houses, putting masking tape Xs on

windows, and battening down the hatches for a slam-
ming hurricane, I got more excited with each degree
drop. Luckily I was not alone. As the pressure dropped
and the eye of the storm neared, we went up to bed.
Over my lover's naked shoulder, I watched as whole
blue spruces blew by the skylight, seagulls flew by at 180
mph, wings straight out, and smiled until she said,
"Honey, you seem distracted." The eye had passed.

During one fabulously low pressure system that
stayed and stayed, we were doing and doing what lesbians do in bed and a big white light hit me in my solar
plexus so hard that it threw me onto my back. When I
opened my eyes, in the corner of the bedroom, high up
near the ceiling, I saw a door with light streaming from
behind it. The door opened and the apparition of my
dear departed mother walked out through the light, in
the wool tweed coat she wore to daily Mass, in her
beloved shoe boots with the worn spot from genuflect-
ing. She looked very cute. She looked down on both of
us, paused, looked me in the eye, nodded her head
slightly, then turned and went back through the door. It
seemed to be her blessing, but maybe it was nothing
more than a nod that said, "Not bad."

Later on the nightstand, I found $1.15 in nickels.

icesKate

1. v. to annoy.

Scientists recently discovered ice on the moon. My feeling is if they can put one man on the moon, why not put all the ice-skaters on the moon?

This antiskating iciness is new for me. Skating used to be so romantic. Hans Brinker skating long frozen canals to glorious victory. It could have been all those dikes. My parents met in high school, skating in the park across from my mother's house. Dad went back to her house to change his skates on their back porch with a bunch of kids. He said that he got horsing around with his friends, an image of my sedate father hard to imagine, and he fell backward off the changing bench and through a window. That was the first time he met my grandfather.

When we were little my parents taught us to skate

on a rink flooded by the local volunteer fire department. My mother fell and broke her wrist while demonstrating an Arthur Godfrey turn. I learned to skate on my brother's hand-me-down black-and-brown hockey skates. Early gender pressure forced me to trade in my beloved two-tones for dorky girl's skates, white with the serrated pick on the front of each skate. That pick flung me to my knees again and again. When sports psychologists are trying to determine why so many men in figure skating are gay, they should focus on that serrated edge for clues. To avoid permanent knee damage, I would lock my left knee, set my left foot on the ice and push off madly with the right, perfecting a skating style that made me look like a human scooter.

My cigar-chomping Uncle Ev worked as a ticket taker at the Erie County War Memorial in Buffalo, and one year got us tickets to the Ice Capades. It was the first time I'd ever gone to a live performance of anything and I was a wreck. At first I completely over-identified with the woman trying to catch the end of the line of girls in Crack-the-Whip. She skated as fast as Bonnie Blair, the gold medal speed skater who went on to star in *Fargo*, but the line of girls rebuffed her efforts to join them. When she caught up, they snapped her forward like some human hockey puck. I sat there with open arms.

Throughout, nervous as a long-tailed cat in a roomful of rockers, I suffered Tina the Ballerina Syndrome.

My grandfather had 45 rpms in color vinyl and when we visited my grandparents on Sundays, I often feigned illness during dinner to be excused to go back to his book-lined study. On yellow vinyl Tennessee Ernie Ford sang "The Ballad of Big John," the pile driving man, a cautionary tale about hemorrhoids. "Teddy Bear's Picnic" was in green. Red was my favorite, however—it was the story of "Tina, the Ballerina."

Long story short—Tina, a little girl, goes to see her first ballet. She's very excited but before it begins, a man comes out to announce that their prima ballerina had fallen ill and would not be able to dance the part. A disappointed hush falls over the crowd. Then, as often happens in contemporary theater, the maestro asks, "Is there a dancer in the house?" As luck would have it, Tina just happens to know the role. She raises her hand and, in a very tiny voice, amidst the hush, pipes up, "Sir, sir, I think I can." Everyone cheers in thankful relief. The maestro, a trusting man, who doesn't believe in auditions or understudies, invites her to the stage. Tina nails all her landings and goes on to become "the belle of Gay Paree."

Ice-skating on TV used to be an event made more elegant and memorable because of its rare, quadrennial occurrence, unlike now when the Zamboni of constant coverage has ushered in an ice age of boredom. The aura of international intrigue—the U.S. versus the Evil Empire, those darned French judges, the threat of defection—

gave figure skating memorable drama. I am amazed at the numbers of names I remember. Peggy Fleming floated, an angel on ice. Dorothy Hamill spawned a cottage industry in hair styling.

My heart broke for *Tai Babilonia*, so Tina the Ballerina. She had grown up through five or six Olympics—first as a spindly preteen in braces, seventy-five pounds, most of that sequins, thrown like a piece of balsa by her partner Randy Gardner. In their last-chance Olympics, she and Randy were second after the compulsories, poised to beat the regal Russian skating pair who bankrupted the Ukraine just so they could have enough flesh-covered body tights with matching skates and chiffon. Suddenly it was announced that my Tai and Randy had to withdraw because Randy pulled a groin muscle doing they wouldn't say what at some after-hours club. I made that up. But I suspected as much. No maestro asked if anyone could skate the part of Randy Gardner, and I was so ready.

Some trace the breakdown of figure skating to Tonya Harding. She did give a new dimension to the phrase "to ice." She rekindled my interest when she skated out for her much anticipated final free-form event and the announcer whispered, "Tonight, Miss Harding will be skating to the music of *Jurassic Park*." Her famous lower lip pout with point to shoelace problem won my trailer park heart.

Nancy Kerrigan skated like she had a candy cane up

her bum. Shortly after the Olympics, officials at the rink where Nancy practiced discovered toxic levels of carbon monoxide. This explains a certain thudding leadenness. Rumor has it she went up to Russian Oksana Baiul— before her DWIs—and said, "You might have the medal, but I've got parents."

Skating went into a decline when they eased the very graceful, former skater Dick Button out of his commentatorship. His coanchor, Jim McKay, gave the basic facts and figures, and sometimes even did it sober, but it was Dick Button, a man so fastidious no one ever dared giggle about his name, who did flawless analysis. The problem came when he was covering the battle of the Brians and practically came during one of Boitano's triple jumps. Dick's Button locked and he squealed, "Fabulous!!!! I'd give it a fourteen."

The networks replaced him with that whining little snot Scott "Every Day's a Bad Hair Day" Hamilton. Nothing was ever right for little Scottie. He bums the girls out. "Oh, she's tired, she's very tired, she's going to fall," and *whack!* she'd slam into the wall in a routine more painful to watch then Admiral Stockdale during the vice-presidential debates.

Another explanation for the decline of ice-skating is that there is too much ice. Florida has an ice hockey team for heaven's sake. That doesn't seem natural. The only ice in Florida should be in bags, on fish, or in ice tea.

Too many skating competitions, exhibitions, compulsories, free styles, singles, pairs, threesomes jam the ice airwaves. Ice dancing looks like the HetCapades. About the only thing the skaters don't do is do it right on the ice. That would be a nightmare for the announcer, even Scott Hamilton. "Look at that, Jim. Still locked, still locked." In every routine, there comes a time for the mandatory pudenda lift. The male skater lifts his partner by the pudenda bone, she does a Superman imitation flat out flying on his palm, about ninety miles an hour down the ice, smiling, lips dried back over her teeth. Perhaps some force of gravity keeps her up there, but I suspect it has something to do with a middle finger, more like those plate spinning things on the old Ed Sullivan show. It's why the brother/sister teams never do well. Doesn't even matter if they are French.

The John Teshification of ice-skating with too many gauzy, maudlin up-close-and-personals ruined it for everyone. "Shhhh, this is the trailer park he was raised in. Look there's a tiny feathered boa. Look there, an old elbow pad. Oooh, look, there's the car his mom used to drive him three hundred miles one way to practice."

I don't want to know. Just shut up and skate.

Every four years.

IoKate

---

1. wherever you are, there ya go.

After the *Provincetown Magazine*'s local police report, "East end man lassoes 300-pound tuna at low tide," my favorite column is by Joe Lazarro. He writes under a pseudonym, a variant of Lazarus. Each week this P-town native brings back to life the town he grew up in. He describes families and natural disasters and old wharves and celebrities. He loves to write and it doesn't seem to bother him or his editor that, from week to week, he remembers almost nothing.

Joe does well to recreate the intangible atmosphere of old Provincetown without the bother of any reliable detail. Most sentences begin with, "If memory serves me . . ." "I have forgotten his name but . . ." "If anyone remembers when it happened . . ." His column is called "Provincetown Memories."

Joe and I have a lot in common. When I review the places I've performed in since 1981, I don't remember details that would interest my dad—like the number of the new four-lane beltway around Lexington, Kentucky. Or the details that would interest my agent—number of seats, percentage split. Or city details for the fellow traveler—best restaurant in St. Louis for an excellent barbecue. When filling my friends in on the details of a just-completed trip, I am left saying to their bewildered faces, "You had to be there."

Brain studies may someday reveal why it is I cannot find my way around a mall without dropping a trail of Carmelkorn crumbs to retrace my steps but can and do remember the most intimate details from a producer's childhood. "Oh, right, wait, wait, I remember! Your father had a heart attack and died when he went to pick you up out of your crib when you were three years old and your mother never talked about him again until just before you had anesthesia for your wisdom teeth. His name was Eugene. Your mother is Pearl. I remember you."

My *Baedyker's Guide* does not serve me except in the most subjective, impressionistic way. Most of the Pacific Northwest, though beautiful, smells like wet paper bags. To avoid tragic overgrazing, most of the populace wears polar-tech that makes men and women look like big warm fuzzy lesbians. Grunge started in Seattle when environmentally minded teens came out of the fashion closet, "Yep, I wear polyester."

Chicago audiences always feel like a big, blowsy, brassy blond. She's on edge, edge of the frontier. It's her last night by the lakes, before she's off west by prairie schooner. She's very rough trade, gangster, flapper, exciting. It could have been the club I often played there, the Park West, downtown across from the Playboy Club, owned by an old Italian family. The owner, Don Something, often brought two of his lovely blond totally turned out daughters to my show. They took turns sitting on his lap in the raised tiered gray leather banquettes, faces lit by table lamps. Perhaps the club made the audience raucous and lawless, but even in Unitarian Church basements they felt that way from the beginning.

I forget where it was, but one evening during an after-dinner program that was dessert, coffee, *aperitifs*, and me, I was almost mauled by a ferocious lesbian. In the early eighties, fancy dinners, with men and women in tuxedos or three-hundred-pound sequined dresses, were an organizing tool. People had been drinking mint juleps at see-and-be-seen Kentucky Derby Parties all afternoon. Some had napped and sobered up before dinner. Others had not. The dinner was oversold, food was running low, so someone gave the signal to double the drink strength. Everyone jacked back into action.

As I began to perform the partiers were not pleased

with the entertainment interruption and there was much exaggerated bug-eyed shushing of each other. When I said the word "dyke," it roused a lesbian in a floral print 6X muumuu, a steel-gray pageboy haircut, shades of Sarah Caldwell. She lumbered toward me as gay men tried to stop her. They dangled off her like ball fringe. She swatted them off, thundering, waving a gnarly Sam Ervin finger, declaiming, as she bore down on me, "I'm the oldest living lesbian in the continental United States and I resent the use of the word DYKE." She stopped short of the stage, glowering at me, but then, triumphant at having made her point, she turned and gallumphed back to her seat.

As I took a deep breath and continued, the power went down, not in a total blackout, more a brownout that made me sound like a very distant and anemic Rudy Vallee. My manager, Trudy Wood, gave me the head-nodding-hand-rotating international sign to "keep talking." I had no intention of stopping. I was going as fast as I could, praying that soon I'd be sipping my own double strength tall one, sitting in a high-backed wicker chair, before they even noticed I was gone. I was speed talking, yelling actually, when I got to the word "dyke" again, at which point the power came on, so instead of merely saying the d-word, I screeched it. Twice as loud. And it hung there, all caps.

Up she came again, the oldest living lesbian in the continental United States, each syllable marked by a thudding footfall as she swayed toward me. I kept talking. Gay men threw themselves on her, "Oh Sarah, sit down for heaven's sake." She flicked them away and glared at me. Table linens got tangled in her muumuu as she shambled through aisles. Centerpieces dropped over table edges in her wake. She reached me, tripped up the small podium step, and crashed to the floor just as I finished with, "Thanks for coming out, good night!" I never looked back.

The last time I ever worked on New Year's Eve was very early in my career in some lowslung, Diane Arbussy church hall, redecorated for the evening's festivities. People were so wasted, I did the countdown at 11:45 and was back at the hotel in time to see the ball drop.

One producer in another city forgot to tell me that I had to perform on the set of a community production of *Shirley Valentine*. He'd gotten a deal on the hall. He said he could rotate the stage to give me a kitchen in England or a beach in Greece. My choice. Since it was Mother's Day, I chose the kitchen. During the show, I felt my mother come up the steps from the basement to stand behind me. Two women in the audience claimed to have seen her.

I love to perform in Canada and used to perform one night in Toronto and the next night in Ottawa, but the difference between the two—cosmopolitan and urbane to federal and uptight—caused such schizophrenia in me that I stopped the sequence.

Going into Canada makes me nervous enough. It's as if I have some hideous criminal record to hide or I'm smuggling hazardous materials into the country. When the customs agent asks, "Are you bringing gifts for friends?" I say no and feel horribly guilty. "Are you carrying any dangerous weapons?" I always want to point to my tongue. I begin to panic at least an hour before the border, knowing that there is a good chance, under Checkpoint Charlie pressure that if they ask me my name, I could very well blurt out "Kathleen Anne Marie Clitoris."

I also love performing in the Bay Area. Though I don't remember the name of the hall, I remember exactly the feeling in my legs when an earthquake rumbled, rattling the huge chandelier still netted from a recent big one. The glass began to tinkle wildly, sending still-skittish audience members into the aisles and toward the exits.

It wasn't until someone yelled "Earthquake!" that I knew what had happened. I thought it was the caffeine. I had had a cup of the Bay Area's finest before the show, and for someone still drinking red bricks of Taster's Choice House Bland, it gave quite a jolt. Stagehands in the wings said it looked as if each floorboard in the stage were part of a suspension bridge that someone had whip-snapped from end to end. When my knees buckled, my first thought was "Must be that cup of jo."

"Earthquake!" immediately jolted me into action. I became the high school English teacher on duty in the auditorium during a fire drill. "Please remain calm. Do not run toward the exits. Stay where you are. While I see what's running down my leg."

At that point there was an aftershock, which, to the unquaked, is a way of saying "another earthquake." Again I called for calm. Then I made a huge mistake. I asked, "What shall we do now?" Never do that. Never ask a traumatized group of one thousand lesbians what to do next. It became process hell. The women in the codependent area were tortured because, while they supported me and my work, they felt it best if they left the hall. A voice yelled from the balcony, "Can we come down and take their seats?"

I broke into a rendition of "The Memorare," a Catholic prayer that I usually used for sound checks. It works well for aftershocks too. "Remember, oh gracious virgin Mary, that never was it known, that anyone who fled to thy protection, implored thy help, or sought thy intercession, was left unaided . . ." It's a lovely long five-minute prayer and I did it in under thirty seconds.

The next night I performed in Los Angeles, or so I'm told. It was a complete out-of-body experience, with me idly wondering, as I was talking, if the old theater had been earthquake proofed, if the wall sconces would break, if the balcony would hold.

When I am asked if I have favorite places to perform, I say in my most politic way, "Your town." Over the years I have learned to have no expectations. One would expect that performing in a huge sold-out 1,200 soft-seater theater with an exquisite sound system would be more fun than performing in a small southern church basement to a crowd disappointingly small because the promoter had decided to contact the media psychically. But the huge hall's red velvet curtains and high ceilings sucked up the sound of laughter and my night on that stage was one of the loneliest nights of my life. The audience that got the psychic call, on the other hand, was in desperate need of some news about their lives and the show was magic.

Thursday night crowds are over-the-hump crowds. They are confident they can make it through the week, so they go out. Friday night crowds are tired from their long week of work and from going out on Thursday night. Saturday night crowds are rested and bumptious. All federal and state capitals are uptight and paranoid. And they don't want to hear about politics because they live it all day long. Each city has a personality, a je ne sais quoi quality, inexplicable to others, but within seconds of being on stage I remember, "Oh, right, Philadelphia."

One of the best shows I ever did was in Santa Cruz about two weeks after the big earthquake. One lesbian had been killed when a wall collapsed on her. The audience came in and for many it was the first time they'd seen each other since the quake. There was much shrieking and hugging. I had taken three detours over the mountains from San Francisco to get there and felt like I was on a USO tour. The show was in an old jazz club unharmed by the quake. The glass on some of the black-and-white promo pictures of the jazz greats was cracked, but the photos had been rehung. The show had a jazzy hysteria, a survivor's fragility, a desperate humor. I felt like the old musicians on the wall were channeling through me. I did comedy all people could dance to. You had to be there.

mastiKate

1. v. to chew food with one's teeth, not someone else's.
2. phr. you are what you eat.
3. phr. Donner, party of one.

Jean Harris was an early hero of mine. Who hasn't wanted to blow away a diet doctor? The headmistress wasn't wicked or whacked out on phen phen, but she did have her reasons. Ms. Harris did go on to do some excellent literacy work while in prison. Her weight remained unchanged.

For my graduation from high school, my parents gave me a doctor's diet. (Some people are not in favor of dieting, but I defend people's right to diet and have actually done clinic defense work, escorting people into Jenny Craig.) Every Wednesday, I would report to my doctor's office and in the weighting room with suburban women, later called "soccer moms," we would take off extra sweaters or layers, headbands, any jewelry, circle pins, brooches, watches. In my case, my eight-pound high school ring was jettisoned before going into his office.

Without a "hello, how are you" exchanged, I stepped onto the white scale under the judgmental eye of his bow-tied slightness and watched as he primly maneuvered the ballasts, hoping those damned little arrows stopped before swinging too far to the right. I thought lite thoughts. Held my breath. When the scales steadied at the fifty-pound arrow, it was an accomplishment.

After the weigh-in, before the vitamin B shot, there was a lecture. During one sermon, he asked me if I knew why the flames of hell burned so hot. Trick questions, like word problems, have never been a favorite of mine. No, Dr. Jonathan Edwards, why *do* the flames of hell burn so hot? After a pause, he said, "Because of all the fat." Years later I heard that he was addicted to speed and had lost his license.

Every day for a month, on his proscribed diet, for breakfast I had a small glass of orange juice, no pulp. For lunch, a piece of cheese and a hot dog. For dinner, a dollop of cottage cheese, a lean ground beef puck, and a leaf of iceberg lettuce. For dessert, Colgate toothpaste. Every day, same thing. It was a steamy July, season of outdoor barbecues and white carbs in mayo. I estivated in the cool basement. One day, as I was crawling up the steps to answer the phone, I had a vision. There at the top of the stairs was God, and she looked a lot like

Audrey Hepburn. So much for the lives of those saints. They were all on diets.

By the end of the first month I had lost thirty-five pounds. Everyone congratulated me. My discipline and self-control were widely praised. I got down to 132 pounds—the average weight for my height according to Twiggy's actuarial charts.

After a month of visions and doctor's visits, I went off to work as a counselor at a Catholic, all-girls', summer sleepover camp, my first time away from home. Each day started with Mass in the pine chapel on the misty lake, then swimming and hiking and other activities, an evening program and then, after we'd put our dear little charges to bed, made sure they were asleep, the fun began.

Some of us would sneak out and meet on the basketball court on starry, balmy nights. I fell in love with everyone. They fell in love with me. Unfortunately, we were Catholic girls. So instead of each other, we ate peach cobbler. We raided the kitchen or the canteen for chocolate cakes. And schnecken—swirly sticky cinnamon buns, made by the large hair-netted German cooks from the little farm towns around the lake. We ate and ate. We said it was all that fresh air.

When my parents picked me up at the end of the summer, my mother took one look at me and burst into tears. On the way home in the car, she told me, "You'll never have a boyfriend if you are this heavy." I thought,

"Promise?" So began my afterschool special love affair with Hydrox cookies. Milk sucked through them. Whole rows of them.

Weight awareness was not new for me. Whenever my crusty, irascible, and very well-corseted Aunt Anna visited, she would look at me and say, "Kathleen, you've gotten sooooooo big," holding that long o, while she looked me over, like I was some sort of budding zeppelin. My otherwise sensible father often expounded on his theory that there was a gene for big buttedness. Only the lucky ones got to be nurses. There was teasing from my brothers. They had high-speed metabolisms and after-school sports and ate huge quantities of anything. I suspected I had a thyroid the size of a pea and only one quarter of it was operational. I walked by a banana and gained weight.

Body chemistry was a mystery to me. Nutrition classes consisted of large slabs of nuns telling us that our bodies were Temples of the Holy Ghost. Our basement was a temple filled with my brothers' musty football, track, and baseball equipment.

I knew my way around a Chubbette department, generally hidden upstairs in department stores behind the Buster Brown corrective shoe department. This was before Stoute Shoppes, or fashions for the Stylish Forgotten Woman or even Triple X Files. Now there are sizes like 16 Petite, which is not a dress but a tea cozy. I grew up in the era of sheath dresses.

My first true retail trauma, however, came when it was past time to retire my trusty navy blue Jantzen with the white piping. It was old. I looked down at the icon of the diving girl and she was on a walker. Following the hygiene instructions from the petitely perky, helpful store clerk, I put another navy blue Jantzen with white piping on over the large white Carter underpants my mother bought for me. I looked down. Under the fluted white skirt my legs were a Rand McNally map of Illinois—blue veins indicating interstates. I had no idea Illinois was so hilly. In the mirrored triptych of the dressing room, under lights that make Caucasian skin look like day-old chicken at Food Lion, I perfected a move I still use. I only looked at my hair.

Coming out certainly made me more comfortable in my skin and I did shed my protective layers and got down to my fighting weight. I learned how to handle a hungry man. Though I discovered my true appetites, I still have food issues. I don't eat Cheetos, except in rental cars. I love to chomp and drive and, when my fingers are the same color as Strom Thurmond's hair plugs, I wipe Cheeto residue off my fingers onto the passenger seat. It's a rental; go mental. Brunch buffets, steam tables, and sneeze guards induce gag reflexes. I order tap water at Eat All You Can Buffets. Thanksgiving dinner, a meal you do not chew, usually frightens me with its showy excess. I prefer an L-tryptophane drip.

With genetic engineering, I don't have food issues. I have trust issues. The great food chain of being has been dropping some links lately. The slippage started with the first person to say, "Great fish, Bob. It doesn't taste like fish." Foods out of season don't inspire confidence. I don't want to eat strawberries in February. Or corn on the cob. Tomatoes are no longer succulent, heavy orbs in late summer. Now they are tasteless reddish plutonium nuggets with corners, available year round.

Anything I might have learned in nutrition classes has changed. Now there are even fake foods. Faux foods. There's TCBY—this can't be yogurt. No one seems to question what it is. I Can't Believe It's Not Butter, a confusing double negative, also comes in a spray with Fabio as pitchman. I suspect he uses it in his hair, or on his Doubting Thomases English Muffin.

Olestra is a new fake fat that has nasty side effects but is already in use. It sounds like the huge tragic Greek opera, where the fat lady got her start. "She sang the part of Olestra beautifully."

Although all my clinical trial data is not in yet, I believe that I will be able to prove that much of the violence in this country is caused by toxic levels of NutraSweet. Second-generation sweeteners have been developed on the backs of poor obese mice. People for the Ethical Treatment of Animals have been trying to unionize the mice and have even appointed a bleached blond spokesmouse with spiked hair who squeaks, "Stop the Insanity!" at rallies.

Whatever the outcome of my research on this mere shuttle we call Earth, the topic is weight or actually weightlessness. Not the slo-mo, hair-waving tethered float of daring doomed astronauts in space. Almost daily, next to stories of food stamp cutbacks, Hudson meat recalls, and North Korean famine, are stories of weight loss among politicians, replete with before-and-after pictures.

The feeding frenzy in the press produces empty calorie sound bites about the president's trainer, the Speaker's new treadmill. Pop psychologists digest the news and produce analysis lite: if they can control their appetites, they can control their parties. Perhaps the press is just jealous, because after all, they languish in the land of snack and fast food on the fly. CNN's Wolf Blitzer is looking a little jowly under that beard. Is he banging back Table Talk Pies he snuck onto Air Farce One?

Everyone is on Oprah watch, gleefully looking for telltale signs of slippage or gainage. "Has he really lost weight, or has he started to dye his hair?" The market runs through binge-purge cycles, with Alan Greenspan monitoring like an abstemious diet doctor. Washington, D.C., home of the people who brought us fat chance, has become like a summer weight-loss camp. Press releases begin, "Hello Muddah . . . Hello Faddah." When political candidates are asked why they want to run for office, they respond correctly, "I'd like to lose some weight."

Beagle-faced former speaker of the House, Tom Foley, worked out so much, he completely ignored his duties and lost his Speakership to the adipodal Newt Gingrich. Now everyone wants to avoid heavy issues of global warming, police brutality, and due process in favor of lightweight quality of life issues—pooper-scoopers, squeegee guys, and readable signs.

If all politics is lo-cal, I have some suggestions:

- GOP, lose the elephant.
- Instead of the Democratic, Republican, and Independent Parties, let's have the Endomorph, Ectomorph, and Mesomorph Parties.
- Instead of spokespersons, let's have the trainers talk.
- Richard Simmons for Health and Human Services.
- Jenny Craig for Secretary of State.
- Change that anthem to "O'er the land of the fat-free."
- Change New Hampshire's license plates to "Live fat-free or die."
- Hold all political conventions at health spas.
- Provide tax write-offs for tummy tucks and liposuction.
- Replace scales of justice with bathroom scales, balanced budgets with balanced meals, arms reduction with redux, and World Banks with food banks.
- "A skinless chicken in every pot and a treadmill in every garage."

In 1974, before dieting masqueraded as decision making, and moral fiber was confused with high fiber, Adrienne Rich wrote, "The decision to feed the world is the real decision. No revolution has chosen it." I've started carbo-loading for the revolution. Pass out that cake.

mediaKate

1. v. to be a Happy Medium.

When I appeared on the *Oprah Show*, the topic was comics helping people with their fears, an idea ripped off from a Comedy Central show called, *C.O.D.—Comics on Delivery*. Oprah acknowledged the petit larceny and then did it better. She assigned each of four comics his or her own ordinary fearful person case.

One woman was afraid of spaghetti and Dom Irrera talked her through her pastaphobia. Dave Coulier backed up a woman who was afraid of going backward. Steve Price counseled a woman who was frightened of her Mr. Fix-It husband. My assignment was a woman, Cathy Schwartz, who was terrified of public transportation. Given that she lived outside of Minneapolis in a town of 1,200, her fears seemed to have more to do with the great unknown than with the great unrode.

The *Oprah Show* flew Cathy to New York City for the first time in her life. My job was to take her on the subway. When I told my friends my task they howled, because they know that when transportationally challenged, I will take a cab.

In addition to helping our charges, we four comics appeared live on the show. Oprah asked each of us about our own phobias. The comic on my left answered that he was afraid that he might come on to Oprah. I was afraid of the same thing but said that I was afraid of arena mascots. I could actually care less about the San Diego chicken; I just like saying "arena mascots."

My real fear is of people saying or doing stupid things on talk shows. Until Ellen DeGeneres was on *Oprah*, I had never watched a whole daytime talk show. I am able to watch nighttime talk shows because they are supposed to be stupid.

The fragments of daytime talk shows I have seen have never been from a seated position. The shows make me so uncomfortable, I have perfected a kind of talk show walk-by, stealing glances, catching a phrase, "Your Momma never smelled right to me." I generally stand in a doorway expecting an earthquake measuring 6.2 on the stupid scale. Why I ever thought I could work on Rosie O'Donnell's daytime show is beyond me. It was a George Plimpton moment in my career. After six months on Rosie, I went on to play goalie with the New York Rangers.

Besides an inability to watch daytime talk shows, I never watch myself on TV. Thankfully most of the shows I have done coincided with the invasion of a country and the show was bumped. "She's on TV again, let's invade something." It's not causal. It just so happened. Ted Mack's *Original Amateur Hour* with my church's bell choir? Korea. My childhood solo debut on *Ed Sullivan*? Killed. Also Korea. Johnny Carson? Vietnam. David Letterman? Grenada.

A friend assured me that TV can never capture the essence of a person, but I find my own image on TV disconcerting. I am like the sister from another planet watching myself on TV. Even though I know it's not true, I assume that what you see is all there is.

One night in the early seventies, when George Carlin was on Johnny Carson he did lots of political material about the Vietnam war. He didn't get huge laughs, but he plowed on and then went and sat on the panel with Johnny who said, "Wow, pretty serious stuff." Carlin explained that he could have talked about kitties and doggies but decided, since he had the opportunity to speak to five million people, he'd do political stuff and try to say something. It was a choice.

Political material has a short shelf life and tends to date a show, so performers are advised to stay away from topical stuff for reruns, even though the host's opening monologue has very specific pop cultural references. They just don't want the comic to do it better than the host. Go figure.

The night I did the *Arsenio Hall Show* no country was invaded and the show did air. Lea DeLaria had been the first out lesbian on Arsenio's show and they were still reeling. "I'm a biiiiiggg dyke!" was still rattling around in some of the studio light fixtures. Arsenio had given her a great introduction. He said other shows wouldn't have her on because she's a lesbian. He said, as far as he was concerned, "it's not what you do lying down, it's what you do standing up." He challenged the audience to be like him and show how much they liked her. Lea came out and killed.

Arsenio must have taken a lot of flack for Lea, because he was tentative with me. I was standing backstage listening to him say something like we all do things we don't like, "Here she is, some bad medicine, Kate Clinton." I wanted to smack him.

It was during the gays in the military hearings, so I chose to do material about them. My jokes sailed right over the heads of the woofing, barking, fist-churning out-of-towners who were in the audience. They were mostly puzzled, except for two apoplectic codependent women fans in the audience who tried to make enough crowd noise for everyone and in the process scared the people around them. Afterward, I was the most talked-about performer in the bathroom; I don't think that's a bad thing.

In six months, Arsenio was off the air. I think I was part of the last desperate efforts of a dying man and the women on his staff to be liberal and controversial. Causal? I have quite a record. The *Joan Rivers Show?* Gone. *Women Aloud with Mo Gaffney?* Gone. I volunteered to do the *Rush Limbaugh Show* just to see if I could get him off the air.

Try as I might, some shows I have done have continued. I did the *Maury Povich Show* twice, although only one of them aired. Not because of any invasion. The Outband, a gay country-western band, did a song called "I'm Hog-tied Over You," with nary a hint of sheep being nervous, but the producers got nervous, declared the song offensive, and would not air the show. The show that did air was far more offensive. In the interest of fairness and balance, the producers gave time to some tired, right-wing Bible-quoting, nutbucket from Michigan. I got a very big gay vibe off him. During the show, a friend of the showpiece fundamentalist, who traveled everywhere with him, stood in the audience and harangued at me, "You would never even be on this show if you weren't a lesbian." Given that the topic was gay performers, he was probably onto something. Maury turned to me and devil's advocattily, asked, "Yes, why are you on this show?" I did my best hurt, huff, high horse and said, "We were told we were going to meet Connie Chung."

Equal Time with Mary Matalin and Jane Wallace was big on balance. Roger Ailes, the producer, Republican pollster and Robert Altman look-alike, give or take fifty pounds, wanted to have opposites, a liberal and a conservative, and while the two women did have different opinions about most things, they enjoyed each other so much the zingy edge between the two of them dissipated into a chummy playfulness. Jane, an earthy veteran reporter, chuckled through most of the controversy the tight-lipped Mary Matalin tried to stir up. Mary was like every cigarette-smoking, Catholic high school bad girl in a rolled-up school uniform skirt that I'd ever had a crush on. After she introduced me, she warned me that she was a practicing conservative, Republican, and Roman Catholic. I paused and said, "I'm wet." Old Jane blew out a mouthful of her beverage and never really regained her composure for the rest of the interview.

Sometimes attempts at tension and controversy backfire. When the topic was gay entertainers on the *Rolanda Show*, the segment producer had a group of fundamentalist churchwomen bussed in from Long Island. The women were all so thrilled to come to the city for the day for an all-expenses-paid show and lunch, that by the end of the show they were standing up arguing with the homophobe in the audience, witnessing about how much they loved their girlfriends and the rest was nobody's business. It was as if the Long Island Libertarianettes had been bussed in by mistake.

Generally I never tell my friends when I am going to be on TV. After all, many of the shows have a special warm-up person who teaches the audience how to clap. Chest high and twice as fast as normal. Even though I have mixed feelings—shame and guilt—about talk shows, I do them because a young lesbian activist once told me that she was home from college on Christmas break, severely depressed, isolated, and alienated. She said if she could have gotten off the couch, she would have killed herself. As she was channel surfing, she saw me on the *Maury Povich Show* and paused. She said she laughed at my Connie Chung line and for the first time thought she might be gay. You never know when a comic delivers.

obfusKate

1. v. not to ask, not to tell.

If my family had been on the *Titanic* when it went down in the cold, dark Atlantic, the last thing I would have seen before the waves washed over my dear father's head would have been a wink. I come from a family of winkers. Entrances, exits, touchdowns, laundry, communion, accidents, minor and major. We all wink at each other. It's a wink audible over the phone. It's conspiratorial, gives a sense that we are in this together, though no one knows specifically what any wink means.

The winking goes along with my family's "don't ask, don't tell" ethic, an old Clinton tradition that our distant cousin, President Bill Clinton, used to resolve the problem of gays in the military.

Not that gays in the military are new. That they are a problem is new. Two words—Gomer Pyle. Throw in

Sergeant Bilko and what the heck, Jamie Farr. In fact, by the time of M*A*S*H, gay was so old news, television-aries had ventured into the area of cross-dressing.

Gays have always been in the military. Alexander the Great was originally Alexander the Fabulous. A gay man invented C-rations. He claims he could never talk anyone into the cilantro garnish. Obviously, gays were not allowed to design the outfits, because we never would have stayed with the earth tones for so long. In the Persian Gulf, for in-stance, we would have gone with beige sand tones.

Military camouflage is about as successful as military intelligence. When you're driving down an interstate and a military convoy goes by, you see it. No one ever squints and says, "Hon, do you see something over there?" "No . . . no wait, now that you mention it, I do see some shaved heads bobbing along." We would have been able to make camouflage work. We are, after all, experts at camouflage.

Gay men have always been in the military. Women in the military should only be lesbians. We would dis-cuss and debate things so much that we would never get around to having a war. "A war? Not with these cramps." "Invasion? You get the beaches wheelchair accessible and maybe we'll talk." "A war in October? What about the softball banquet?"

When history is written, it will be revealed that some right-wing mole was at all of President Clinton's press conferences after the election and, in the afterglow, kept shouting, "What are you going to do about gays in the military?" As Bill was stopping for coffee during his morning jogs, the mole was there in sweats, "What's your feeling about gays in the military?" That guy kept bugging Bill until he had to answer, and in a nationally unguarded, unpatriotic moment akin to dragging a burning flag across the Vietnam Memorial on Veterans Day, the new president said that he thought gays should be allowed to serve in the military.

At which point the Joints of the Chiefs of Staff went out. The Very Irritable Colin Powell led the reaction by claiming that gays would destroy the military. Promises, promises.

Old soldiers never die; they become military experts and go on CNN. The gays in the military controversy came along at a perfect time for the military, not just because they were downsizing and it was an ideal way to get rid of workers, but because at that moment we were plumb out of wars for old soldiers to be expertizing on. They had been an indispensable source of fill during the Gulf War. Technically that was not a war, it was an operation, Operation Just Cause. We don't have wars anymore; we have operations, an unexamined source of high costs in managed scare.

"Operation Just 'Cause George Bush Felt Like It" was not the first time that a president kicked off a re-election campaign with an invasion. Nor will it be the last. I was so upset by the operation that I went down to

Washington, D.C., for the anti–Gulf War march. It was not a very exciting march. Straight people don't know how to march very well because they don't have to do it as often. Gay people, lesbians especially, are out marching all the time. We have "Take back the day," "Take back the night," "We'd like a little bit of the morning if you don't mind," marches.

But the queer contingent was fun. One of my favorite signs was the acronym L.A.B.I.A.—Lesbians Against Boys Invading Anything. Even though there are not many words to rhyme with Saudi Arabia, we had some very good cheers. "Read my Labia! U.S. out of Saudi Arabia."

The march almost took the stigma out of being one of the supposed 9 percent of the population not supporting the war. It was a fine march, until we got in front of the White House and my girlfriend, who believes that a bullhorn is a sexual device, shouted, "Die-in!" That is a signal for everyone to hit the pavement in a mass symbolic death. It was a cold day in spring and I was wearing a new coat. So there were all my comrades sprawled about on Pennsylvania Avenue and me standing like the Washington Monument hissing to my crumpled girlfriend, "This is a camel hair coat! Screw supine!"

With the issue of gays in the military in the news, the old soldiers were back firing all over the airwaves. Senator Sam Nunn, Little Miss Fistula, held hearings and one day even took everyone on a field trip to a submarine to prove how close close quarters really are. He could just have shown *Hunt for Red October*, a movie I saw on a crowded airplane; I thought I would perish of double claustrophobia.

The hearings were yet another circle jerk among the ethically challenged. Nunn made no sense when he tried to prove that cramped quarters are a huge turn-on to many gay people the world over. I know I love to bang my head on low ceilings during sex. My favorite moment came when Senator John Kerry of Massachusetts explained patiently to Senator Strom Thurmond of Mars that straight people do sodomy too. The orange-tinted octogenarian fired back an indignant, "They DO NOT!" and in that moment revealed just why he had so much time to spend in the Senate.

It all seems to boil down to bathrooms. Every civil rights movement has a bathroom moment. The Disabilities Rights Movement? Bathroom accessibility. The Black Civil Rights Movement? Bathroom sharing. The Equal Rights Amendment? Anti-ERA forces said that if the amendment were passed there would be unisex bathrooms. This panicked people who had apparently been raised in households very different from mine. "Don't go in there! That's the men's bathroom in this household." No women could even be elected to the Senate until bathrooms were built for them, lest they have to excuse themselves from an important hearing to go to Bethesda to find a women's room.

The gay rights movement bathroom moment was

specifically about towel-snapping gay men in showers. At first I was disheartened that the whole issue of gays in the military was reduced to porcelain, but then I thought it was good, because it meant we had arrived as a genuine civil rights movement.

"Don't ask, don't tell" might be a nice ad campaign for *The Crying Game*, but it's no way to live a life, or run a military. The government is asking and telling and pursuing gay people right out of the military. The winking at legally sanctioned discrimination costs $23 million a year, or its equivalent, three hammers.

After the furor over gays in the military died down publicly, and the witch hunts escalated privately, it became clear that the military was no place for women, either. According to the findings of Professor Anna Simmons, an assistant professor of anthropology at UCLA, the post–Cold War era might seem like a perfect time for women to be in combat units. In her column in the *New York Times*, "In War, Let Men Be Men," she summarized some of the things she discovered during the year and a half she observed elite twelve-man A-teams in the marines.

She claimed that women in combat actually endanger our troops. Why? Because GI Janes inhibit male bonding. It is this male bonding, she said, that enables men to survive the stress of working closely under the difficult conditions of cramped space, long hours, hardship, and extreme danger.

I expected Professor Simmons to say something like "counting pushups with each other promotes male bonding" or "shouting encouraging things to each other promotes closeness," but no. Men build trust by bragging about their sexual conquests!

What's up with that?

Simmons says simply that GI Gals make the GI Guys self-conscious about claiming to be all they can be. The presence of women, especially Demi Moore, makes men either clam up about their reputed prowess or shtup to the task of backing up their boasting. That interferes with the bonding process and thus destroys critical unit cohesiveness and combat readiness.

Admittedly I was not having a Phi Beta Cappucino when I read her article but I thought I missed something in Professor Simmons's column. I looked back. Did she say her degree was in Anthro-apology? Was she making excuses for men behaving badly? Boys will be boys, the penis with a mind of its own, they can't help it, et cetera.

I'm no Margaret Mead (although one Halloween, I did dress up in sensible shoes, a lovely wraparound sarong over my regular clothes, bangs, and a big walking stick), but from what I've seen in Aberdeen and other military trials, I'd have to conclude that it's time to get men out of the military. Shut down Fort Brag. It's time for eunuch cohesiveness.

In war, let women be men; in peace, let men be women.

playKate

1. v. to accessorize with nasal dilators.

The great Yogi Berra once said, "The more the people hate politics, the more they love their sports." National political cynicism is at an all-time high. An actually lame, lame duck president who injured his knee on a golf junket, garnered a 60 percent approval rating. When he does nothing, we approve.

Sports have certainly taken some critical hits though—the baseball strike, the O.J. trials and denials, Atlanta's Olympic Park Bombing, Tonya Harding hiring hitman Sean to whack Nancy Kerrigan's knees, biters Mike Tyson and Marv Albert. In the same week Nike was found to be running sweatshops in Vietnam, thirty-one members of the Heaven's Gate cult left their vehicles behind wearing nylon sweat suits and sneakers emblazoned with the Nike swoosh, like a big check on the final check-off list. Sports public relations firms cranked into high gear to refurbish Nike's image and to get people to stop making those damn "Just do it" jokes.

Despite setbacks, American sports still has its Super Bowls, World Series, cups, green blazers, roses, rings, trophies, plates, and domed stadiums. Sport has become an international gladiatorial bread-and-circus diversion for spectators able to buy tickets or work a remote.

The main sporting rule I adhere to is an odd/even, butch/femme formula. In an even butch year I enjoy football, boxing, weightlifting, and other brutish, large muscle, spitting sports. In odd, femme years, I enjoy chess, tennis, gymnastics, synchronized swimming, and other finesse, small muscle schvitzing sports. I never enjoy bowling or monster truck shows.

Another self-imposed sport rule limits me to watching semifinals and finals. I have neither the time nor the interest to watch baseball from televised college draft picks to spring training to the end of the season. This apocalyptic, end-times, self-imposed confinement of sports viewing has been necessitated by twenty-four-hour sport channels that cover all sixty-four rounds of the U.S. Tennis Open and every hole of every golf tournament.

As a rule, I watch sports with the sound off, unless it's Monica Seles. Most sports announcers are such blowhard pronouncers and speak as sports clairvoyants who know how players feel just by the way they lean over at the foul line. "Well, Jim, he is feeling tired, look at how he's bent over, hands on his knees, but he knows this is do or die time and he has to reach down deep within himself for what it takes to make a heckuva play." Or they can tell what golfers think as they line up putts. "He knows he has to sink this putt, Trevor, to get the prize money for his sister who needs a heart, lung, liver, and spleen transplant."

I was born on the cusp of Title IX, a time when, according to the sports pages, only men played sports. Yogi Berra never said that about sports and politics. It was me. While I'm no fabulous sports babe, one of my career goals, besides writing comedy that all people can dance to, is to be a sportscaster. Bo might know baseball, but I know a couple of things as well.

Golf

When CBS sportscaster Ben Wright claimed women don't make good golfers because their "boobs" get in the way of their swings, I thought, "Two words, Ben. Beer. Gut."

For some of my friends, nothing is more relaxing than watching golf on television, but all those guys whispering brings up painful memories of how my family dealt with problems. "She says she's a lesbian," whispers one commentator. "A what?!" whispers another. "A lessssbian, shhhhh, you'll scare the horses."

No matter what they tell you in those dioramas in the golf museum in St. Andrews, Scotland, the game of golf was actually invented in 1953, by two housewives in West Palm Beach, Florida. The two women were neighbors. One morning while they both were hanging up laundry, they caught each other's eye over the clothespins and the flapping sheets. One thing led to another and before you could say "Shout it out," they were in the Danish Modern master bedroom suite of one of the women.

That was washday Monday. Same thing Tuesday, Wednesday, Thursday, Friday, but not Saturday. Nor Sunday. Because their husbands were home. They got together again on Monday, made love in the four-poster Stickley on the Dan River percales of the other woman. Then they talked.

"What are we going to do? How are we going to get them out of the house?"

They thought.

"Well, we could give them each a stick and a ball and tell them to go out and hit it around in the backyard."

"Nah, they'll never do that."

"Oh okay. A stick, a little ball, and tell them they have to hit the ball in a hole."

"They'll never fall for that. Besides they'd be back in no time."

"Okay. A stick, a ball, and eighteen holes."

"Hmm. That'll take longer."

"Yeah, we'll dress them up in clothes of colors not found in nature. Tell them they can ride around in carts. Take showers together. Drink beer and talk about every single shot they took."

"It's worth a try."

And *that* is how the game of golf was invented. True story.

Basketball

My high school girls' basketball team was unheralded and undefeated. It was the years of the three-dribble rule in girls' basketball. After three dribbles, a player had to pass the ball. Most of the girls on my team had learned to play basketball with their brothers and could give dribbling clinics at halftime, so the three dribbles made the game slow. A Valium Invitational.

Only one player on a team was allowed to run the full length of the court. Or was thought to be able to do it. She was called "the rover" or "lesbian." Nonrovers skidded black skid marks to a halt at the mid-court line. Since I had learned to play with my brothers on our long, narrow driveway court, I had a great outside shot and was good under the basket. Although I didn't think so, others, especially referees, thought I played "too rough." My coach sent me in for hatchet jobs, and I usually fouled out before the game was over.

Our high school had been built in 1920 and had no gym, but it was located catercorner from the War Memorial where the Syracuse Nationals played before they moved to Philadelphia and became the Seventy-sixers. We practiced on that buoyant wooden floor whenever we could. Since we never knew when it would be available, we never had the right equipment with us and often played barefoot in our blue plaid box-pleated uniforms until the Nats showed up for practice. On some glorious days our practices overlapped, and I got to play with Bob Cousey. He called me the Barefoot Contessa.

Nothing helps pass the time more in a long northeast winter than watching women's basketball. Now we can watch it year round, thanks to the new women's pro leagues. The WNBA games are much more fun to watch in person, though. The televised games seem to be produced by the same people who covered the 1989 San Francisco earthquake and managed, during ten days of coverage, never to mention the words *gay* or *lesbian*. The WNBA games show endless shots of Phoenix coach Cheryl Miller's beautiful hair weave. They studiously avoid any loving pans of the celebrity row lest they inadvertently out someone as a basketball fan. In a roiling sea of short-haired women fans, they focus on the one dozing father and his bored-looking son. Sometimes, after a fabulous I-love-this-game play of the week, they mistakenly flash to a bevy of square-bottomed lesbians high-fiving in the stands and it's a quick "Camera Two!" back to Cheryl's weave.

I never watch women's basketball with my gay men friends. One Easter, after we'd eaten ham pinioned with pineapple rounds and ripped out our fillings with marsh-mallow peeps, I turned on the women's NCAA basket-ball finals. As I tried to watch, my gay friends dished the coach's fashion sense, "What was she thinking with that floral print on national TV? And a capped sleeve? Not in the nineties."

Baseball

Baseball is one of the few sports in which the coach wears the same outfit as the players. Thank goodness. George Will, the prissy bow-tied pundit, prattles endlessly each spring about baseball as a metaphor for life's lessons. The homily on the day the twelve-year-old fan scooped a home run ball out of an Atlanta Braves outfielder's glove in the World Series and helped the Yankees win must have been on man's inhumanity to man. Or cheating. De-spite my fondest wishes, the "C.R." on those baseball hats stands for Colorado Rockies, not consciousness-raising.

I didn't think I was a baseball fan until the Yankees and the Red Sox were in the playoffs in 1976. I had moved from Boston to upstate New York to teach and that fall I must have used the teams as compare and con-trast writing examples one too many times. The school where I taught was going through an accreditation process and all classes were being observed by state officials. I had warned my class, especially a young turk named Steve, that it was imperative they get to class on time.

The day my class was observed by the accrediting team, a large Sister of St. Joseph sat in the back with a pen and a checklist. It was the day after the Yankees had beaten my Red Sox in a late night, late inning thriller. My New York class was gloating palpably when as usual Steve arrived late with an entrance that was a dazzling mix of Kramer and the Fonze. He'd completely forgotten that the class was being observed and did not see the hulking black presence of Sister Mary Credit squeezed into a corner desk before he spoke. In support of me and to forestall my admonition, he squared off and pointed his finger at the class, and as he panned the class he slowly punctuated, "The fuckin' Yankees suck." As he hit the word "suck" he spotted the nun.

He looked at me and I told him as sternly as I could, "Steve, you need to apologize to the class for what you said."

Without a second's hesitation, he punctuated again, "I'm sorry I said 'suck.' Twice." And sat down.

The baseball strike and the fans who found something else to do in the interim showed the lessening of baseball's hold on the national psyche. Analysts, including curious George Will, blamed the strike on greedy players and owners, but I blamed it on Ken Burns and his forty-seven-part baseball series on PBS. People who watched the whole thing felt that they had just about enough of baseball thank you very much and turned to *Lucy* reruns or lawn care.

Though I quit watching baseball to spend more time soaking my perm rods, I look forward to a professional women's fast pitch league and still play the occasional pickup game myself. After I came out, I played one season on a women's softball team. It's required. My favorite part was after the game—the babes, the beer and broaster hut. We had the usual differences of opinion. After several long wrangling meetings, we settled on purple-and-red uniform shirts. No one seemed to know what puce looked like.

Some members of my team were fierce frustrated athletes; others were "not into competition." They were the ones who usually showed up with ten-inch cleats. Most of the season our pitcher was not speaking with the catcher because they were both seeing the same woman, our shortstop. I played third base and spent most of my field time praying that my shins would not be shattered by line drives. I keened "please don't hurt me please don't hurt me" in a wail that was quite disconcerting to batters. Our coach was mortified by my behavior until their pitcher walked in three runs.

In right field we had a woman who was a therapist. As a right fielder, she was a wonderful therapist. She was very supportive of the team. Whenever a fly popped up to center, she could be heard saying to the center fielder, "I believe in your skills; I support you in your effort to catch the ball." We didn't have a winning season, but we did have the best parties and made lesbians

more visible in the small farming community where we
played each week.

Track

My brothers were all varsity letter track stars. They an-
chored relay teams and ran dashes, and my younger
brother was a great long distance runner. I preferred
night running in the neighborhood. I had read Jim Fixx's
book about running before he died, and I slowly worked
my way up to a long slow slog through three miles. Time
was not the object. Sweat, getting my heart to bang out
of my chest, and gasping for air were my personal goals.

One day I was running after school and the head of
the athletic department saw me slogging around the
track. Based on that spectacle he asked if I would coach
the girls' track team. Schools were just starting compli-
ance with Title IX, and there weren't enough qualified
coaches, so I was a natural. For some reason, I said yes.
It seemed like a good idea at the time. I had no idea
how to work a stopwatch. I figured if you made it
around the track you deserved a medal.

On the first day of practice, also the day of a late
spring blizzard, 156 girls showed up. We had to practice
inside, in the same room as the archery team. Having
track practice with the archery team is a good way to
get the numbers down and gives new meaning to making cuts. The shortest girls always wanted to do the high

hurdles. The lightest girls wanted to throw the shot put. The girls with asthma wanted to run the sprints.

While my own limited coaching skills did not make for a winning season, some natural athletes excelled and won state championships in spite of me. Nonetheless, I will always be grateful for track because it gave me my first after-dinner speaking experience.

The high school's year end sports award banquet at the local country club was a marathon, mind-numbing affair that lasted hours because varsity and junior varsity letters and trophies in all fall, winter, and spring sports were given out by monosyllabic coaches shell-shocked to be out of their nylon warm-up outfits. They seemed lost without their whistles. The awardees were not always the brightest of bulbs, but that did not stop them from attempting Heisman-trophy-quality acceptance speeches thanking their parents, coaches, teachers, et cetera. I sat correcting practice English Regents exams and trying not to heckle.

The audience of parents and friends was nearly co-matose by the time I got up, second to last, to say a few words about the track season and give out awards. By that point, four and a half hours into it, with dinner a faint memory, it was almost time for breakfast. I greeted them with a simple, "Hello, sports fans," and the audience laughed out of sheer relief.

Since then I have spoken at lots of dinners. After a few hours of speeches many of them have that same sports banquet snoozy lethargy, compounded by an open bar. Once I was invited to roast Colorado's Senator Pat Schroeder before she retired. There were lots of heavy hitters to do the roasting, but the idea of a roast was lost on them and instead of roasting, there was respectful eulogizing poaching. I sat with Senator Barney Frank and after the tenth reverential testimonial thudded the crowd into a stupor, he looked at me and said, "We are so golden." When I got up, I commended Ms. Schroeder for all her snappy comebacks and suggested if she ever ran again that she print her campaign slogan on the tear-off paper on sanitary pads. The audience snapped to relieved attention.

Some of the worst sports dinners I have ever worked were fund-raisers for the Gay Games in New York City. Before I came out to my dad, I told him that I was going to the G-Games and tried to slur my way through it. By the time the Games were held in New York City, I was out to my dad and when I told him I was going, even though we were on the phone, I could hear him think, "The Gay Games? What in God's name are the events?"

I explained that there is the triathlon for gay men. Tanning, brunch, and tea dance. And that there is also an event called the Sperm Carry, an event for women that involves small artichoke jars and running from borough to borough. The medal is awarded based on number and motility of sperm at the end of the day. He told me to cut it out.

As payback for appearances at Gay Games fund-raisers, I was asked to host the opening ceremonies. Not until I arrived at the Stadium on the day of the event did the organizers tell me that hosting meant that besides announcing the teams as they marched onto the field, I would also have the honor of introducing Rudolph Giuliani to the crowd. The mayor had just authorized massive cuts in AIDS funding and he was about as popular as ACT-UP at communion time in St. Patrick's Cathedral. I went down to the field, out onto the platform, and announced, "Unfortunately, John Cardinal O'Connor could not be here to bless the athletes, so please welcome the mayor of New York, Mr. Rudolph Giuliani."

If you reviewed the videotape you would see me then turn and practically run over the mayor as I tried to get off the platform amidst a chorus of boos and shushes. You could also see that at no time did I ever call him "Adolph" Giuliani, which his office claimed when they objected to my emceeing a dinner where he was to appear as well. I might have thought it.

Emceeing the dinner was difficult because organizers were worried that Giuliani would be heckled and that he would hector right back and a food fight could ensue. The dinner was huge and had the feel of a large open-air gay mosh pit. The mayor was late. Suddenly the organizers, who'd been stalling, got a signal on their headsets that he'd arrived. They high-signed me to take the microphone and settle everyone down.

Everyone sat, except for this big schlump of a guy who kept walking through the crowd. I thought someone should urge him to find a seat, then I realized that it was the mayor. He was uncomfortable but didn't lecture too much, and only one person held up a protest sign. My girlfriend. When he left the podium, I got up and couldn't resist saying to his receding form, "Now that wasn't so bad, was it, Mr. Mayor? You're just lucky that one of the groups that was going to be here didn't show up. They call themselves GALIB—Gays Against Loehmann's Invading Barneys—and they'd like a word with you."

Tennis

Bud Collins, the bearded sports commentator of tennis, should have been a professional golfer. His loud, mismatched Madras outfits scream golf, Sunday afternoon tee time. One time when he caught Chris Evert in the tunnel at Wimbledon after a loss to ask her an annoying up close personal question she cut him off with "Nice pants, Bud" and walked on. He did once announce, "Two great women on grass—it doesn't get much better than this." I couldn't agree more, but suspect I might have added a bit of topspin.

Billie Jean King, with her never-say-die dive for more balls than a Chinese volleyball player during a cultural revolution style of play, was loud and inspirational to me.

She was so much more fun than the stoic largeness of Margaret Court or the gamine precision of Virginia Wade.

More than birthdays, I mark my age in generations of women's tennis. First Billie Jean. Then the breakfast at Wimbledon, Chris Evert–Martina Navratilova duels. And finally the Steffi Graf, Monica Seles years. When Monica was stabbed by the crazed German fan who wanted to help Steffi stay in the number one seed, he cut short a fine career and some fine tennis sound effects. It got so that I would just turn on the TV when Monica was playing, crank up the sound, and listen in the bedroom. I often wanted a cigarette after a long rally.

When Martina Navratilova came out to Barbara Walters without shedding a tear, tennis got even more interesting. She and Chris Evert showed the dynamism of gay/straight girlfriends. And Martina was a needed moral voice in sports. She had nothing to lose—no product endorsements, no plum commentator gigs be-cause she was an out lesbian, so she spoke out.

About the time Magic Johnson announced that he had AIDS, Wilt Chamberlain claimed to have slept with more than ten thousand women in his book *My Stilt Never Wilts*. That works out to about 15.4 seconds per woman and indicates an extremely thoughtful lover. Mar-tina said in an interview that if a woman claimed that, she would not be labeled a stud; she would be called a slut.

All of us on Martina-watch cheered. When it was

announced that Martina would speak at the 1993 March on Washington, we cheered again. Besides emceeing for an hour at the end of the March, I was doing color commentary for Pacifica radio and their producers snagged speakers and performers off the stage for us to interview. When Martina strolled over to our table, I lost the ability to talk and my cohost, the ever garrulous Larry Benski, took over. Martina smiled graciously. I did manage to invite her to a party we were throwing that night at a local hotel.

I alerted one of my most rabid sports fan friends that Martina might come. This friend is a proud old-time butch and could easily do commentary in any sport and often does, with facts and figures, complete with enough deep background to drive you to distraction. Bud Collins has nothing on her. The party was mobbed and in high gear, packed and overflowing out into the hallway, when a buzz went through the crowd. There was Martina, with a gang of her gorgeous friends. She got stuck in the crush in the hallway, next to my friend, who smiled cooly at Martina and said, "You that tennis player?"

Martina smiled back, "That lesbian tennis player."

Football

Of all sports, football seems to be the most sanctioned homosocial opportunity for straight men to be with each other, pat butts, struggle, strive, and take showers together. All that talk of tight ends and penetration.

The reason there are face masks on those helmets is so they can't kiss each other.

Since my memory doesn't store football statistics, I can't remember the number of the rainy mid-seventies Super Bowl that first revealed to me the sexual nature of football. It was before AstroTurf or the climate control of domed stadiums. It was muddy like a football game should be. According to the excitable announcer, John Madden, some team's all-star defensive player, named either Bob or Dan Seaman, was having a "heckuva day." I could not have been watching with my brothers or my father or I never would have heard, "It's really slippery out there! That Seaman is everywhere!" the way I heard it. Maybe his name was Dick.

I grew up with football. There was no league for me and my girlfriends, so we organized a powder puff league. The number of serious injuries sustained suggested more gun powder than powder puff. For sixteen years, I organized a family touch football game on Thanksgiving Day at the local grammar school field. The invitation featured a pen and ink drawing of a football with drumsticks on a platter, garnished. For sixteen years, on the Friday after our Turkey Bowl, I was unable to walk. My mother still insisted I go shopping with her. We now play x-treme charades.

My father went to college on a football scholarship. My brothers all played Pee Wee and high school football. Meals were scheduled around their practices and games. My mom prided herself on her ability to Shout out grass stains. The laundry room still smells like dirt, exertion, and Clorox.

In the early nineties, a woman's antiviolence project released figures that showed that spousal abuse occurred more often on Sundays during football season. The study did not go so far as to theorize that the violence was actually frustrated sexual energy. But I think it is. It was a very controversial study and Katie Roiphe, conservative columnist and antifeminist hack, jumped all over it and said it was completely false. Shortly after, Nicole Brown Simpson was found dead, slashed to death next to some bloody Bruno Magli shoeprints.

Perhaps there were some problems with the report. But I know from personal experience that during football season on nongame or nonpractice days, after dinner dishes and cleanup with my brothers was a full contact sport with vicious towel-snapping. That was when I first developed snappy lines as self-defense. If I could make them weak with laughter, I had a chance.

Since the O.J. trial confirmed my suspicions about football, I have not watched the game with any enthusiasm. My partner, disdainful of most television, loves to watch football and during the season I always know where she is on Monday night. The sound of Frank Gifford's voice makes me go directly to sleep. I have spoken to people in sleep disorder clinics about the effect. Kathie Lee must be very rested.

pontifiKate

1. v. to speak while wearing a Melitta filter on one's head.

Some people remember exactly where they were for different assassinations or assassination attempts. I remember exactly where I was when Sinead O'Connor* tore up the picture of Pope John Paul II on *Saturday Night Live*—Madison, Wisconsin, at the home of Teresa Sprecher, a founding member of Fallen Women, one of the oldest women's production collectives in the United States.

Fallen Women was started in the late seventies to produce women's music concerts. The collective began with ten or twelve women but had dwindled in recent years to four women who would produce shows when

---

* No relation to, and not the lovechild of, Sandra Day and John Cardinal O'Connor.

ever they got a hankering to see somebody again. They liked me and I always loved seeing them, catching up on what had happened in the year or two since my last visit. New careers, new locations, new loves.

Many of my road friendships are like that. Twenty-four hour visits, intense, no time to waste talking about the weather, unless it is catastrophic and they or someone close to them has gotten hurt. We spend only a few minutes on frivolous details before we cut to the chase. This intensity of friendship often causes problems with my longer residential friendships. Even when friends tell me to relax, and remind me that I'm not leaving tomorrow, I don't do well at "hanging out."

The members of Fallen Women were all former Girl Scout leaders, now college financial directors, preschool teachers, print shop owners, all with the requisite cabin "up north" that they built themselves. They were all solid citizens of the community—on teams, in study groups, on committees, in volunteer groups, with full work weeks and fun weekends. It never failed when I was with them that I would become excruciatingly homesick for the life they all seemed to have.

They had produced shows together for so long that they were an efficient, smooth-running team. They could get the backstage cleared, security paid, volunteers thanked, hall cleaned, lights down, sound struck and packed into Honda station wagons in one hour after a show and have you home by 10:30 Central Stan-

dard Time with pizzas decided on and ordered. I'm talking well oiled.

After the years of being billeted in community
housing, I had grown to prefer a good anonymous Red
Roof Inn. The only exception was when I stayed with
the Fallen Women in Madison. There was always a
woodstove throwing heat, extra slippers, and best of all,
the special BarcaLounger. What could be better? We
were catching up on eighteen months of news, chomp-
ing on Midwest pizza, with the TV on in the background, muted. I always made them watch Dennis Miller
and the news of the week on *Saturday Night Live*, during
which they groaned but were unfailingly tolerant in def-
erence to me, "Shhh, she's doing her homework."

Over Teresa's shoulder, I was keeping an eye out for
Dennis, when Sinead O'Connor came on and began to
gut her way through a song by Bob Marley, "Until the
philosophy that holds one race superior and another in-
ferior is finally and permanently discredited and aban-
doned, everywhere there is war . . ." In her final keening
wail, she pulled out a picture of Pope John Paul II and
ripped it right down the middle.

We all sat stunned. Even I, who had been working
to pump up my sacrilegiosity quotient, was amazed at
my reaction. My heart started pounding and I expected
either the floor to open to hell or the stage lights to
come down right on her darling bald fontanel. Volume
up or down, it was the rip heard round the world. Were

we running low on pictures of Pope John Paul George Ringo? Did Sinead rip up everyone's favorite picture? Had someone misplaced that negative?

The next week, *Saturday Night Live* guest host Joe Pesci announced, as if anyone had asked him, that if Sinead had done that when he was host, he would have slapped her. The crowd went wild.

Everyone had a love the sinner, hate the Sinead reaction. Even Madonna weighed in on the negative side. That was rich. A woman who often put a crucifix where you really shouldn't, complaining. She was just jealous she hadn't thought of doing it. Her career was plateau-ing. Her limited edition, spiral bound, *Sex* book had been out and dissed (what? no pop-ups!?); she needed the next new thing and along comes this upstaging little papal pic-tearing Irish waif.

It was as if Sinead had tried to take a Polaroid of Mother Teresa just as she stuck her tongue out to take communion. The whole incident showed that as popes go, John Paul II was popular like baseball's Mr. Perfect Attendance, Cal Ripken. But, as popes go, he was not my favorite. The pope who won my heart appeared in *Rabbit Test*, the only movie Joan Rivers ever made. Instead of doing annoying appearances to the gathered multitudes, he had a pedicure while one of his minions crouched behind the papal balcony waving a mockup of the pope on a stick. Now that was a pope.

John Paul II had taken over for the Laughing Pope

who only laughed about XXXIII days and then died. Food poisoning, they say, but there was always a hint of scandal, bounced checks, arsenic in the incense, whatnot. The Laughing Pope had taken over for the big Eating Pope, John the XXIII, a hulking kindly guy, a bit like Paul Prudhomme. Or Dom DeLuise. John XXIII was pretty much a homebody, so he convened the Vatican council to modernize the church and had a couple of cute young priests open the windows to let in some fresh air. Many people like myself enjoyed the fresh air so much, we continued right on out.

So the new Polish Pope, the Skiing Pope, was called in to restore order. He donned the Melitta filter about the same time Reagan was inaugurated. The Pope and Reagan. Forgive and Forget. As with Reagan, there was also an attempt on the pope's life. He recovered but I always suspected that when he was in the hospital, the Disney people came in and reconditioned him. I always suspected the same about Reagan.

The big appeal of the new pope seemed to be that he was able to move on his own. He hiked, he walked, he rollerbladed, but the streets in Rome were too hilly and cobbled. He had his own sport-utility all-terrain popemobile but he really loved to fly and it showed. He had more frequent flier miles than Secretary of State James Baker during a Mideast diplomacy marathon. What a shuttlecock! The pope kissed a lot of tarmac.

Every time he brought one of his tours to the

United States, I volunteered to open for him. I prom-
ised to waive my usual fee. My agent never put my best
foot forward, however. In preparation for his appearance before thousands of teens during the Worldwide
Celibacy Tour in an open field in Colorado, organizers
vacuumed prairie dogs out of their holes to make way
for the thousands of Prayery Dogs that summer. One
woman who worked security for that visit said they were
not allowed to call the thousands of outdoor toilets
around the perimeter of the field Porta-Johns. They
were told it was offensive to Pope John. So they called
them Vati-Cans.

Although millions of dollars were spent on each papal road show, money that could have been spent on
the poor who were rapidly inheriting the earth, I preferred John Paul II on the road. When he was home
padding around the papal residency in his ermine-lined
papal mules he caused even more trouble.

In addition to his home chores of saying Mass, running meetings, making saints, and the annual spring
cleaning of his disciples' feet, when the pope was home
he accomplished more than Martha Stewart on crystal
meth. He revised the Baltimore Catechism, got his own
phone line, cut a CD, wrote letters, a new book. Busy,
busium, busiorum.

The pope had the Catechism, the baby-blue-and-
white Q and A book of my youth, updated with the sins
of the modern era. Very hip. And very helpful. If you

are running low on things to do, sins to commit, it's loaded with suggestions. One very surprising upgraded rule: it is now a venial sin to make faces at your phone answering machine, if the person leaving a message is someone you don't like.

To review: a venial sin is a little mark, a schmutz on the soul. It can be flicked away by saying a few little prayers, aka ejaculations, always a very confusing penance for my adolescent brothers. Some days in the Catholic Church are a lot like double coupon days.

Under the pope's leadership, the Catholic Church got a new 900 number. At first I imagined heavy breathing, the pope talking low like Barry White: "Hello, my name is John Paul II, and I'm touching my ciborium right now." But it's a number you can call for movie ratings and reviews. Can you say Fathers Siskell and Ebert?

Plans are in the papal pipeline for confessional call-ins, 1-900-MEA-CULP. "Thank you for calling His Holy Hotline. If you are calling from a rotary phone, please wait for one of our handsome young prelates. If you want a non-English-speaking confessor (and don't we all?), press 0 now. If you're calling from a Touch-Tone phone and have never done this before, please listen to our entire menu of sins before beginning. Press 1 for mortal sin. Press 2 for venial sin. Sin of Pride? Press 3. Gluttony? The pound sign. Anger? Gently press 4, et cetera. For your penance, press star and wait for the tone."

The pope wrote a blockbuster best-selling book,

called *Crosssing the Threshold of Pain*. I loved the spiral
binding. The tongues of fire foil cover was a nice touch.
And the part about the summer he spent with Mother
Teresa, "Terri," at Castel Gandolfo was surprisingly hot.
It was translated from the Latin, *Ego Sum Okay, Vos Est
Excommunicatus*. In the foreword to the book, there is a
Vatican disclaimer that Pope John Paul II is no relation
to RuPaul. His Extreme Roundheadedness wrote each
evening after his meal in response to questions submit-
ted to him. The book is so realistic, on some of the
pages there are even kielbasa stains. Some of the faith-
ful claim to have seen the face of Jesus in the stain. But
when I squinted, I thought it looked more like Bobby
Vinton.

The book was a huge hit and did so well in Libris on
Tapis, that the Vatican merch-meisters put out a CD of
the pope humming along to the rosary. Listening to that
CD on scramble in my car disc player and to a CD of
the Benedictine Monks singing Gregorian chant and
Dominique, the Singing Nun got me cross-country in
only 148 days.

His Very Narrowmindedness does it all, and he finds
time to write letters! And not cryptic E-mail. Big letters. He sent one letter to the U.S. Conference of Bish-
ops before his "I'm No Pedophile Tour." I don't know if
he was expecting trouble or he'd been corresponding
with John Cardinal O'Connor, who had been having

trouble with the Irish Lesbian and Gay Organization (ILGO). They wanted to march in the New York St. Patrick's Day Parade and, of course, carry their usual "Tongue me I'm Irish," "Suck my sheila-laugh," "Cunnilingus is not an airline" signs. Even Andrew Sullivan was not able to mediate the dispute. The pope felt compelled to write ahead, in a letter called "No Promo Homo," to tell the Bishoprics that they could not condone anything that was supportive of homosexuals.

Even I got a letter from the pope. I was impressed by His Thoughtfulness, even after I discovered that he had sent a letter to every woman. The Nixon stamp was an inspired bit of whimsy. It wasn't one of those pray-or-else chain letters. One of those "Don't be like Mrs. Eulah Banks of Okra, North Carolina, whose husband, Wilfred, was tragically crushed to death in the compactor of his self-owned trash vehicle because she did not answer her letter in time." No. This was a letter of apology. Talk about letter bombs! The pope explained that sexism is a sin and then apologized for any inconvenience the stained glass ceiling might have caused, and by the way, still no deal on gal priests.

Lots of churches are trying to clean up their apse before they feel they can send out the big party invites or order up the millennium party platters. In the Netherlands, eight hundred Germans apologized to some baffled Danes for the Nazi invasion. The Southern Baptists apologized to African Americans for any part they might have had in slavery or contemporary racism. African Americans everywhere were not quite relieved, but played Tracy Chapman's lyric, "Sorry is all that you can say," in acknowledgment of the gesture. The Jesuits apologized to women for any oppression they might have been party to—frightening a number of coeds at Boston College.

The Catholic Church, after much study, even ventured that they were wrong for locking up that solo-centrist Galileo, or dissing Darwin. What's next? After looking at videos of Shannon Lucid's hair in weightlessness, they released a new papal letter, an apology to Sir Isaac Newton entitled "Gravity! Who Knew?"

But one thing I learned in the church is you can't just say you're sorry; you've got to do some things. Penance builds character. So they better accept my bid to produce the big 2,000th birthday parties for Jesus Christ. You thought the Tall Ships were big. They already know me from my offers to open and proposals to hook the pope up with the summer Lollapalooza Tours. I'm proud of that one. Lots of merch, good outfits, huge crowds—it's a natural.

For the Big Birthday Bash, I'm thinking Surprise Party, but I'm really leaning more toward "Jesus Christ! This is your life." He's sitting in a nice chair, listening with his eyes, a little puzzled, to a pleasant offstage voice: "You and I worked in the shop together. You could get a square peg in a round hole." I'm trying to talk Mary into coming back. She does not like big events. She just doesn't go in for the big appearances anymore. She's more backyard, lawn chairs, New Jersey. She's a lot like Jackie O in that way.

If they accept my bid, I might tape my picture of the pope back together.

prevariKate

1. phr. liar, liar, pants on fire.

The day Richard Nixon took the big dirt nap in 1994 was Earth Day, and a minor earthquake rattled Southern California near his burial site. I've always thought it wasn't so much an earthquake as the earth doing "Ptui" to get rid of him. Nixon was buried in San Clemente, French for "without a pardon," near the Nixon Liebrary.

Presidents Ford, Carter, Bush, and Clinton made the service look like *Four Presidents and a Funeral*. I don't remember if Ronald Reagan was there, but neither does he. The first lady, Pat Nixon, or "Poor Pat" as she was usually referred to, was not there. She had predeceased her husband by five years. Who can blame her? Tricia Nixon Eisenhower was a reminder that we all had gotten older. Henry Kissinger mumbled through his eulogy, sounding like Marlene Dietrich doing "The Man I Love."

The funeral was another event in the long Nixon rehabilitation—he got us out of Vietnam (he did not), he started talks with China (it was the only country that would talk to us at the time), and the Watergate break-in was ordered by Hillary Clinton. It was an astounding bit of revisionism.

Nixon is dead! Long live Nixon as Newt Gingrich and his band of Republican House majority tricksters. The GOP hired O. J. Simpson, Kato "Pretty Street, No Cars" Kaelin and Lance "I saved Jay Leno's career" Ito to focus attention out west, away from the right side of the country while they dismantled the government in one hundred days or less, by taking out a "Contract on America." My theory is that Nixon ordered it from the grave.

But I get ahead of myself. I began performing stand-up comedy in 1981, the same year that Ronald Reagan began his comedy. The president was known as the master of the one-liner. His gigs were well produced and spun by a professional atmosphere queen, Michael Deaver. Security was a problem, and after the assassination attempt on Reagan, Alexander Haig did not reassure us with "I'm in charge now" from a White House Situation Room/Tanning booth.

After he was shot, Reagan achieved an untouchable

quality. Mustn't make fun of him, hush, hush, he was almost assassinated. My theory is that the Republicans did it. I am not so callous as to suggest they shot him, that was Jodie Foster, but I am suggesting when he was in the hospital, Reagan was reconditioned. Same thing happened with the pope the same year.

Nancy Reagan was such a piece of work, she should have been on my comedy payroll. She seemed so lifelike. It was her Valium-laced frozen face that launched the War on Drugs with "Just Say No." The "thank you" was implied. At one photo op press conference, she toured a crack house and decried how awful it was, yet one suspected that for our Drug Czarina it had something to do with a plaid couch.

I never got used to saying "President Ronald Reagan." It was like saying "President Merv Griffin." Reagan wasn't so much a president as the host. He was having such a good time playing president and going on vacation that he decided to run again. The Democrats nominated Walter Mondale as sacrificial lamb and rightly suspected it was going to be a real rout, so they put a woman on the ticket, Geraldine Ferraro. That way they could lose heavily, then say "I told you so," and not try a woman again for another hundred years.

In his second term, Reagan completed the work of his first term—the rich got really rich, everything was deregulated, advocacy programs were quashed, the Savings and Loan program was trashed, the deficit was tripled, unions were busted, Housing and Urban Development was in shambles, banks were closing, the military got lots of new toys, the religious right was stronger, and AIDS was ignored. This proved that the operation to make Reagan a perfect asshole had been a success.

During his second term, the Iran Contra scandal came to light, with the gap-toothed Caucasian soldier of fortune Oliver North running money through the White House so he could get his own talk show. In what later became the Alzheimer's defense, Reagan claimed he thought it was a war *for* drugs, not on drugs, and that Iraq was the past tense of Iran. He also said he thought it was Pittsburgh, not Bitburg.

Polls showed that people disliked everything Reagan was doing but somehow liked him as a person and thought he should run for a third term. There were rules against that in what was left of the Constitution, so Gramps couldn't run and besides he'd lost interest. The Republican Convention was held in Houston in August, so that Republican women could wear their furs in the air-conditioning and nominate Vice President George Halcyon Bush.

My dad said George Bush seemed like a nice enough guy with lots of experience—senator, ambassador, head of the CIA under Nixon, vice president. I argued he just couldn't hold a job. Head of the CIA was the scariest thing on his résumé. When Curious George announced in the most emphatic tone he'd ever used that he didn't eat broccoli, never liked Broccoli, that even Bar couldn't make him eat BROCCOLI, I half suspected every time he said broccoli he was giving someone the signal to invade another Central American country.

When George Bush got the nod from his party he announced his running mate, a true comedy gift, Dan Quayle. Even though Doogie Quayle made Bush look downright presidential, he was not as unnerving as his brittle wife, Marilyn, who always gave the impression that it was really Lily Tomlin in there (still looking for signs of intelligent life in the universe). Dan went on to become a spokesman for Cliff's Notes and was himself a wonderful speaker. During one address to a Rotary Club luncheon at the Cincinnati Golf and Country Club, he quoted Rodney King, from the Los Angeles riots, "As Mr. King once said, 'Why can't we all get a lawn?' "

The Bush/Quayle ticket went up against the Dukakis/Bentsen ticket. Mr. Charisma Bypass, Michael Dukakis, lost me in the presidential debate, when CNN's Bernard Shaw asked the first question, "Mr. Dukakis, if your wife, Kitty, were raped and became pregnant, do you think she should be allowed to have an abortion?" When Dukakis did not jump over the table to punch Shaw out or say something like, "How dare you even put that idea into words, you little weasel," he lost me. Instead, the bloodless wonder, Dukakis ended up talking about drug kingpins; his campaign started warming up that tank.

Once he became president, George Bush revealed a

vein of Styrofoam and no matter how deep he tried to go, he always ended up bobbing on the surface. His inaugural speech was like being present at the death of language, the original Dead Poets Society. After the Reagan years, there were only three people of color in the Republican Party. Their slogan was "Republicans— the Other White Meat." George Bush tried to dispel the "whites only" image of his party, often referring to his Mexican-American grandkids as "the little brown ones over there," and nominated Clarence Uncle Thomas to the Supreme Court.

All went smoothly during the nomination process of Clarence Thomas until Anita Hill came forward with her sexual harassment charges and was put on trial by the so-called Ethics Committee. Arlen Sphincter, of Pennsylvania, read his favorite passages from *The Exorcist*. Utah's Orrin Hatch looked as if he'd sat in something. And Joe "Hair Plugs for Men" Biden kept the proceedings going and going so long, I half expected to see one of those pink Energizer bunnies banging the drum slowly down the table.

Bush's approval ratings slipped. The election was drawing near. What to do, what to do? He started flexing his Commander in Chief muscle and invaded anything. Panama; Operation Just 'Cause George Felt Like It. Somalia; he should have sent in salad shooters. Saddam Hussein questioned George's manhood; Poppy went up to Maine, blasted around in his high-speed cigarette boat, thought things over, and finally invaded. It was all televised and managed by Norm Norm Big as a Dorm Schwartzkopf who went on to be a spokesman for the Quality Value home shopping channel.

The Operation was televised by CNN, though it should have been a Sunday afternoon sport show "Shooting Fish in a Barrel." The only good thing about the Operation was that Bernard Shaw was trapped under fire for three days in a hotel in Baghdad. Bush's ratings were boosted for a few minutes, even though he didn't really get the job done because the dictator Hussein is still alive in a bunker somewhere. His ratings hit an all-time low when he puked and landed facedown in the Japanese Prime Minister's lap, talking about jobs, jobs, jobs.

Presidential candidates should be drug-tested. Take it from me, you cannot fly to forty cities in two days and not take drugs. I know they didn't fly through Newark. By the end of the 1992 campaign, George was hanging off the backs of trains, talking about bozos, wacked out on Ritalin. He was defeated by Arkansas Governor Bill Clinton who was speeding nonstop on white sugar and junk food.

After Gramps and Poppy, President Bill Clinton (no relation) was like having your brother as president. He could talk, and after twelve years of pretty wild syntactic rides, it was nice not to wince every time the president opened his mouth.

The first strains of "Inhale to the Chief" had not even died down, though, and I was disappointed in Clinton. This is a lot like saying, "I'm so disappointed in the patriarchy." He backed up on gays in the military, health care reform, Lani Guinier, welfare reform. Whenever he talked, I swore I could hear that backing-up sound trucks make.

When President Clinton announced in a State of the Union address that "the era of big government is over," it sounded like vintage Reagan with a touch of Elvis. When he signed a bill eliminating welfare, just before his second presidential campaign, he made Nixon look like a liberal.

When Bill Clinton ran for a second term, he ran against Bob Dole. After 114 years of trying, Dole finally received his party's nomination because Liddy Dole at the Republican Convention nailed her landings in a fabulous floor routine to the music of "Oh My Man I Love Him So" and created an image of a Kinder, Gentler Bob. All for naught. So few people voted in the elections that the ones who did were called activists. Nobody wanted another old guy president who couldn't talk.

The American people got an unexpected windfall in President Clinton's second term. A twofer. Two presidents for the price of one! One, the numbingly detail-oriented talking policy work and two, a total Babe Magnet. No wonder he lost weight! Despite allegations about his sexual performance, Americans liked his job performance.

The more accusations of sexual misconduct, the higher the approval rating. One wondered how many women it would take to get him to 100 percent.

When President Clinton announced that big government was over, the subtext was that the era of big global business was cranking up. The middle person was eliminated. Despite antitrust laws, mergers continued: CBS and GE, ABC and Disney, NBC and Microsoft, RJR Tobacco and Nabisco, Bill Gates and Martha Stewart until everything was owned by seven white guys, not including Martha Stewart. Smaller players were allowed to buy items the federal government was selling off in an end-of-the-millennium tag sale. I bought a lovely minimum security prison. A friend bought Arizona.

prognostiKate

1. v. to have crystal balls.

(Written when the *Newsweek* "Lesbians" cover story appeared the week after the "Could Dinosaurs Return?" cover story.)

NEWS BULLETIN, the year 8093—Paleoarcheologists have discovered an ancient mosquito suspended in amber resin in a dig outside a known lesbian festival site in northern Michigan. Scientists were studying the foundation of an ancient "eatery," complete with ceremonial food arches, when they chanced upon the find. The excellent condition of the site also enabled them to uncover a small container of carbon foodsticks labeled "Dino-Fries."

Hypothesizing that the lambent mosquito had bitten a lesbian attending the festival, scientists used a syringe found in a diet Pepsi can to extract blood from the mosquito's perfectly preserved and engorged proboscis and isolated an incomplete strand of DNA. They augmented the partial strand of DNA with the DNA from a leather softball cover, circa 1991, and using ordinary tap water, rehydrated the complete DNA and ecce lesbo! A reanimated lesbian.

"This is an extraordinary moment," said project spokesperson Simone Noway, "for it has allowed us to end our centuries-long speculation about what caused the lesbian to become extinct. As soon as 'Amber' came around, we were able to talk to her and find out what happened in those crucial latter years of the twenty-first century."

Archeologists at Hetrick-Martin University had led research in the field for years, pioneering dig techniques at sites all over North America and proffering several intriguing theories on lesbian extinction.

In 7969, "Stonewall Six Thousand," at an East Coast urban site, they uncovered scuffed, but perfectly intact Vibram-soled footwear, "Doc Martens," which still had a half-life of about a billion years. Scientists speculated that their huge, weighted soles made it difficult for lesbians to flee from their predators. "We believe that in some cases, especially in the larger-sized footwear, lesbians undecided on this style looked down at their feet and actually died of fright. The later platform style was apparently quite lethal," said Noway.

In 7890, Western water workers chanced upon the site of the second Lesbian Herstory Archives. The treasure trove yielded up invaluable information from the late 1900s, a crucial period in lesbian evolution. Artifacts found at that site refuted the earlier-held notion that some drastic environmental or climatic change, some hole in the ozone layer ("bigger than Perry Watkins's nose ring"—unclear pronoun referent, but very funny to many at the time), caused the Great Dyke Demise.

After poring over archival information, scientists speculated that in fact the sudden glare of media publicity was too much for the lesbian organism. "After living mushroomlike for years in the primordial ooze of rumor and innuendo, lesbians were sent into shock by the 'Lesbian Chic Period,' following as it did on the heels of the 'Stealth Lesbian Era.' Despite an emergency airlift of cool sunglasses from L.A. Eyeworks, many perished from squinting."

Perhaps the most controversial theory was presented at the 6100th Annual Women's Studies Conference by Professor Mookie McClinton, famous for her ovulal work, "Lesbian Family Trees: The Burning Bush." In her thesis on the Dyke Diaspora, "Lesbo a Go-Go?" she stated, "I believe, quite simply, that they ate their own. And I don't mean that in the good, old way," she added wryly. "It's no coincidence that at that same time, the mainstream, swollen from assimilating many tributaries, overflowed its banks. Not only were food sources destroyed, but weak dykes were blamed. It was *The Hunger* part two, redux, pas de deux all over."

Scientists briefed a slightly dazed Amber, wearing multipocketed pants and a No One Knows I'm a Lesbian T-shirt, very popular in the Irony Age in the late 1900s. She rejected the shoe, sunlight, and snack theories. "NOA," she said flatly. None of the above.

"Here's what happened. Cruises became popular. Especially after the pictures of gay sailors in that military fight. RSVP Cruises started doing submarine cruises. And the Aqua-Separatists sailed everywhere: Alaska—the 'KlonDyke' Tour; Australia—'The Down There Tour'; Lesbos—'The Redundancy Tour.' Not me. I believe a navy of ex-lovers cannot sail. I was actually one of the last land-based lesbians.

"Anyway, they ran out of places to go. At the time of my tragic accident, a mud-wrestling top-bottom thing, I know plans were in the works for a huge cruise to Jupiter. They'd be gone seven thousand years, stop at other planets out and back with a different show every night. There were just that many lesbian comedians then. Lesbian lift-off was scheduled for late 1998. Near as I can figure, they'll be back soon, give or take a month."

rustiKate

1. to attend a women's music festival.
2. six degrees of separatism.

One afternoon in 1986, while I was writing at my desk in Cazenovia, New York, the phone rang. I absentmindedly picked it up and a slightly southern accent said what I thought was "Ka-ate, this is Honest Ed . . ." I immediately began to regret not letting the answering machine do its thing and idly wondered why some used car salesman was calling me, how he'd gotten my number, if he was just working his way down through my small town's phone book.

Then I heard him say, ". . . so, I'm doing a new book in the *Tales* series, and I'm developing a comparison between the all-male Bohemian Grove and an all-women's music festival and I was wondering if I could just pick your brain a little about some details. If now's not a good time . . ."

"Armistead! How are you? I'd love to talk!" and we roared through an hour of conversation and gossip about other writers, our partners, the closet, politics, our families, and finally festivals.

The first time I met Armistead was after a show at the Great American Music Hall in San Francisco. That night on stage, before I could hit a punch line, a huge anticipatory laugh exploded out of the dark. After a few times, I felt desperately predictable and started stalling and speeding up to throw the laughter off track. A couple of times I'd get to the punch a nano ahead of him. The things that made him laugh made me hear my material in new ways. I showed off for him. Linguistically, bodily, gaily. It was a rip-roaring blast.

Afterward, in the basement of the hall, Hunter Davis, a performer from South Carolina, brought down two friends to meet me. One was Terry Anderson, an activist, writer, and radical from Atlanta. He had interviewed me once. When he invited Armistead to make an appearance in Atlanta, they fell in love and Terry moved from Atlanta to San Francisco. He introduced Armistead and I said, "It was YOU!" and he hooted with laughter.

His *Tales of the City* had saved me when my mother died in 1984, the night of another show at the Music Hall. I flew home from San Francisco for her funeral. She had not been well, but I was still in shock. The day after the funeral I had to fly to Seattle to do a show, then to upstate New York to be with my dad. The only way I was able to get through those cross-country flights was by reading a *Tale* out west and a *Tale* back east.

Perhaps it was payback time when he called to talk. I was the right person, that's for sure. Whether I liked it or not, festivals were my middle name. I gave him dish from lots of different festivals and he crafted and contrasted them wittily, perfectly, contrapuntally with the rituals of the all-male Bohemian Grove in northern California. Immediately after we spoke, I panicked that when his new *Tale* came out, my separatist sisters would purplelist me from all festivals in perpetuity. The book came out, and came and went, and no one ever said anything to me about it. I'm still disappointed.

After performing at the Southern Women's Music and Comedy Festival three times, the West Coast Women's Music and Comedy Festival three times, the New England Women's Music Retreat three times, and the Michigan Women's Music Festival one hundred four times, I purplelisted myself from festivals.

Although I did perform at the National Women's Music Festival in Bloomington, Indiana, it is not on my list of festivals to girlcott, because actual buildings with theaters, rooms with beds, indoor plumbing, and dining areas with hot food and beverages are involved.

Smaller outdoor gatherings, however, are included. Women's Harvest in the fall in upstate New York was my very first festival. It always conjures up a vision of pulling women out of the ground by a hank of their hair like organic carrots.

The Poconos Women's Weekend in Pennsylvania was for years produced by a nutty collective of women from Philadelphia, many of whom no longer speak to one another. The Poconos, all nooks and hollers, twists and turns, were hell. Whenever I asked for directions, I rolled down the window, watched the guy's lips move, then pulled out and asked, "Did you get that?" My manager and I were lost for hours once. At last, we found the place. We pulled in but were immediately disoriented by the smell of steaks and barbecued chicken. We knew we were in the right place, however, when we saw huge naked sumo women sliding down a turquoise water slide into the pool.

Despite smaller regional festivals ("My dad has an arid piece of scrubland—let's have a festival!") and the popularity of cruises for wealthy aqua-separatists, the mother of all festivals, "Michigan," goes on. Although it's been in operation for twenty years, no one is able to give clear directions. Signage is a problem since organizers know it's like advertising: "Hey you! Big Angry Guy with the Gun! Yeah you! Over here!"

In January, when I was invited to the twentieth Michigan festival, it seemed like a good idea. But on an unrelenting hot day in August, driving miles of unmarked roads through tufted fields of asparagus ferns, it seemed a hideous idea. Hopelessly lost but making good time, we flagged down an old Buick barreling down the dirt road. The guy driving slowed his car and I thought, "This is how people die."

He smiled warily. I gave the international signal to roll down your window. "Hi, thanks for stopping. Can you tell me the way to the . . ." and I wanted to say "festival" but the f-stop kept my top teeth stuck to my bottom lip; what if he killed me for being a lesbian? What if . . . ? Then I realized he was being wary, because maybe he thought I was, despite my hair, a tourist from the Pacific Northwest where most straight women look like lesbians and he didn't want to presume or insult me. Or maybe he thought I was a lesbian and would kill him.

The pause lasted forever. Dust settled, gritted my lip. I spat out "festival." We both said it at the same time. He nodded wildly and pointed in the direction I'd just come from, gave a few more instructions, gave the accursed "Can't miss it" and drove off.

The logistics—parking, food, sanitation, entertainment, sleeping spaces—all things second nature to Hilton or Embassy Suites, make the festival harder just for the fun of it. The bivouacking babes who make it all happen make Stormin' Norman and his troops look like pampered slackers.

Security and crowd management attract women with control issues and an unnatural fondness for two-way radios. They dispatched us back and forth between Gates A and B with crackled communiqués. As we drove between each gate, we saw a wood nymphish woman in tie-dyed diaphonous all-natural cottons, flower in her hair, dancing a Jules Feiffer homage to Mother Nature. Or she was on acid.

We stopped. She said she needed a ride to Gate B. I wasn't sure what gate we were headed for by then, but I said, "Get in, there's room."

Just barely. The object of the Michigan Festival is to pick up other women who are completely out of the way, saying, no problem. By the time you arrive at the festival gates, you hate your passengers with a blind murderous resentment. We'd already gone out of our way a mere ten hours to pick up a friend of mine in Chicago. She was a masseuse and brought her massive padded pink massage board in case she wanted to pick up some spare change. The festival is like an underground Russian economy after the fall of communism with bartering services and a black market in animal products.

The van was packed. As we were bouncing along, my friend said to the wood nymph we'd just picked up, "I'm Donna, what's your name?"

"Feather Mountain Grace."

"Hey, Feath. Where're you from?"

"The cosmos."

"Really? Me too. What part of Chicago?"

suffoKate

1. nice try, no cigar.

I'm no movie critic, and I don't play one on TV, but if I could change my name to Chantal for just a minute, I'd have to say that something weird is going on. In the springtime of smaller films, I thought I spotted a trend.

The trend probably went undetected because the three movies, *The Fan*, *Celtic Pride*, and *The Cable Guy*, were so unwatched. People were saving up to see the White House get blown up by a giant hockey puck in *Independence Day* or Tom Cruise dangling from a harness in *Mission Impossible*. For those of you who missed the movies, here they are in three nutshells:

The Fan—Robert DeNiro stretches and plays a crazy guy, this time Gil, a knife salesman whose marriage falls apart. Distraught, Gil becomes obsessed with a highly paid baseball player. When the player goes into a batting slump, Gil ignores his wife and becomes, well, fanatic about him and will do anything to help him get back in the groove.

Celtic Pride—When the Boston Celtics get into a seventh playoff game with the Utah Jazz, Dan Ackroyd and a friend, also of a crumbled marriage, get the star player of the Jazz drunk and then kidnap him, all to help their beloved team win.

The Cable Guy—Jim Carrey plays Chip, the title role. His excuse for bad behavior is a barhopping mother who left him every day in front of a TV. When he is asked by a customer, played by Matthew Broderick, to install free cable service, Chip tries to extort friendship as payment with the warning, "I can be your best friend or your worst enemy."

Each plot line, and I use the term loosely, suggests that the motive for mayhem is a failed marriage or a lousy mother, but I think the motive has less to do with women and more to do with straight men's unrequited love for other straight men.

This theory explains why the Promise Keepers are so hot, why there's no rust on Robert Bly's Iron John, and why gay men are so straight. When you try to make straight men who love other straight men get married to women, it doesn't work and often results in obsession, fanaticism, danger, and pathology.

Enter Dick Morris, longtime fan of Bill Clinton, our Celtic president, ready to do anything to stop him from slumping, even kidnap issues from the other team if it will help his man win. He's well connected and cable ready to be Clinton's best friend and then worst enemy. Even when he was with Sherry Rowlands, he was on the phone with Bill. Now that's triangulation.

Sure we could blame it on Dick's wife, or his mistress of eight years, but I think it best if we leave her out of it, especially after her remarks in the *Newsweek* feature on adultery—the one after the one on the testosterone patch for men. The article actually stated that the increase in adultery is caused, not by testosterone speedballing, but by more women in the workplace. You've come the wrong way, baby. In that same article, Eileen McGann, Morris's wife and one and only family value, said that when it comes to Dick, she had been thinking about dismemberment.

Which brings me to cigars. How else to explain their recent popularity? Guys get together and chomp 'em, smoke 'em, compare sizes, watch women with them in their mouths, even have their own magazines about them with Excalibur centerfolds. But they still ain't satisfied.

Perhaps in an attempt to divert my attention from their emboldened love, some straight guys in Congress passed the Defense of Marriage Act and Clinton quickly signed on. Nice try, fellas. Gay marriage is not the way to go either. After all, when *two* guys are from a failed marriage, it's twice as bad.

sindiKate

1. Southern Baptist word for "Disney."

It was midweek. I was on tour in Florida, had never been to Disney World, so decided to go. It was one of the saddest things I'd ever done.

On my first tram ride over the Magic Kingdom, I spotted Goofy waiting on the platform ahead, at the FantasyLand exit. He was standing in the shadows, nodding and waving at tourists getting off or going by. I dreaded the encounter because of my morbid phobia of mascots. I never know where to look; I don't want to look them in their Nerf eyes and talk. I feel silly speaking into their mesh bow ties, trying to see the person within.

As the kids on two trams ahead of us got off in a cloud of marijuana, Goofy stepped forward into full sun, and without squinting, showed them something in his four-fingered gloved paw. They stepped back quickly, tumbling into each other. By the time we got to the stop, Goofy already had them handcuffed and was leading them away. When those kids got busted by the G-man, the total number of kids in the park that day dropped to twenty-seven. The park was a sursurrant mass of seniors in matching windbreakers. Shuffling Sansibelts.

Some people worry about what's happening in Central America. I worry about what's happening in Central Florida—the slow Disneyfication of the world. And heaven forbid if Disney decides to get into the prison business. They've already got too many crowd control skills. I was raised on the pre-Bambi imagery of the flames of hell at Our Lady of Psychological Warfare, and God's afterlife kingdom of heaven, hell, and limboland, so I was never that impressed with the rather wimpy Disney imagery. But now I am frightened.

Disney takes the fun out of fundamentalism and sells it back to us as vacation. Old Walt must have been some kind of control queen. From the minute they place the Haj need in you to make a pilgrimage to either Florida's Disney World or California's Disneyland before you die, the experience is controlled down to the last detail. As soon as you say the inevitable "I'm going to Disneyland!" they take charge of your transportation, housing, food, entertainment. Once you are in the Disney force field, tuned to the Disney traffic network, you are told how to behave.

"Welcome to the Disney parking channel. Park your car as directed. Get into the trolley as instructed. Do not stand in the trolley. Do not hang out of the trolley. Proceed to the ticket booth. You and the whole family WILL have a wonderful stay. Have a nice day." It's a kind of bossy fun fascism. They decide when and how you'll have fun. As a stand-up comic, I understand the impulse to control reactions, to get people to laugh on cue, but I'm no theme park. Yet.

Many people don't believe this, but there was a time before Disney. I was there at the beginning. I was a charter Mouseketeer. I didn't have the ears because my mom didn't allow me to send away for things. Something about not needing mouse ears in God's heavenly kingdom. Disney was one of the first to realize that TV was a great baby-sitter. They broadcast every afternoon in that hour when mothers are trying to make dinner, everybody's tired, and sororicides are most likely to occur. Though my mother was glad to have help with four of us before dinner, she never trusted the secularity of a magic kingdom here on earth. When the tall Tommy Tune Mouseketeer, Bobby, went on to become a Lawrence Welk Show dancer, she eased up a little.

With my brothers sitting cross-legged in front of the TV, we marked the days of the week with Disney. Spin and Marty at the Triple R. Why, on Thursday, you might find yourself on an elephant on the moon, or riding in an auto underneath the blue lagoon. That was the day that was filled with surprises. I was surprised that I was just as interested as my brothers in watching Annette Funicello's breasts fill out her mock turtle Mouse club T-shirt. I pretended to be fascinated with Darlene, but she was too goody-goody for me.

At first there weren't any bad girls in Disney. But then Disney must have done some focus group testing and we got Hayley Mills. Two of her. And the fabulous Cruella DeVille. The first time I ever saw color TV was when a friend, whose father worked for GE, invited some of her girlfriends over to watch *Peter Pan* on their first-of-a-kind color set. While they were all swooning in identification with the dreadfully sweet Wendy, I was smitten with my first female-to-male transfairy, J.R.'s Mom, Mary Martin. She was forty-one when she played Peter Pan. It was before bungee jumping. That night I broke my bed trying to fly.

Somewhere in America, sitting cross-legged in his Mouse ears, was a little Michael Eisner thinking, "When I grow up, I'm going to run this thing." When old Walt died from lung cancer and left the place to his sons, well-meaning but without much between their managerial ears, Disney hit a natural corporate entropic wall. Then, like some latter "here-I-come-to-save-the-day" saint, Mighty Mouse Michael Eisner was there. He brought on fellow former Mouseketeers like Jeffrey Katzenberg with a love for what Disney once stood for, to restore the nap on Mickey's felt ears, and to make a Maxi Mouse out of Minnie Mouse.

They made some bonehead mistakes; Michael Ovitz's $12 million golden parachute comes to mind. Locating EuroDisney outside of Paris was a problem. It quickly became obvious that when people go to Europe they want to see real castles. The Imagineers had not thought of this. At that point, Eisner should have sold it to Boutros Boutros Ghali, then head of the United Nations. They could have converted it into a village for the refugees from all over Eastern Europe. They'd have a place to stay, their own currency, food, and an infrastructure that, as everyone knows, is very important. At the last minute a sheik bailed Disney out. That's the good news. The bad news is that Minnie Mouse has to wear a chador.

Eisner and the Disney Corporation wanted to build a history theme park in Manassas, Virginia, dangerously close to that other Ur–theme park, Washington, D.C. Unfortunately they chose the site of an old slave plantation, which was also the site of the mini-mayhem of Loreena Bobbitt. The "It's a Small World After All" Disno-anthem would not have played well there.

The world did not get smaller when ABC and Disney merged. After all, the Southern Baptist boycott of ABC/Disney for portraying a lesbian as a human being on ABC's *Ellen* was a public relations bonanza. After years of complaining about Mouselini and the Disney-fication of the world, I feel sheepish supporting the DisnoJuggernaut.

But I have thrown myself into the effort. I have installed a GLBT chip in my very high definition color TV that screens out everything that does not have the ABC/Disney seal of approval. I have a new Miracle Ear in my old mouse ears. I have crafted an ad campaign for their fall lineup: "Watch Us and Go to Hell!" I have pledged to sponsor fifty Disney Air Kids scholarships for those who cannot afford the park admission fees. I have adopted a medium-sized town in Virginia and have pledged to purchase as many Disney products as their usual per-Baptist consumption. I have reserved two acres in Perfect World, Disney World's planned community. I know they'll like the Gay and Lesbian Community Center.

vaKate

1. Kate Cod.
2. ant. no vay, Kate.

Here's a tip: never move to where you vacation. The reason you like to vacation there is simple—you are not working. It can be a big mistake, but if you must make it, Provincetown is a nice place to move to. The town is located at the tip of Cape Cod. From Boston by air in good weather, it's a seventeen-minute flight on Cape Air. In bad weather it is forty-five minutes of lurching, white-knuckled hell. By car it's an endless, circuitous two- to six-hour ride. The signs say, without apparent hint of irony, "Provincetown Straight Ahead."

The Chamber of Commerce visitors' brochures do not say so, but Provincetown is the largest open-air manic-depressive treatment center in the world. The off-season population of 3,500 swells to 35,000 in season. Off-season there is 47 percent unemployment, on season 100 percent of the year-round residents work hundred-hour weeks in two or three jobs. Fishing used to be the town's main industry, but overfishing forced fishermen to leave town or find other work. Often that meant converting their modest homes into bed-and-breakfast guest houses, or selling off the family land for development. During a building boom in the eighties, many old Provincetown fishing families caught the quick-money-for-land fever and subdivided their three-story homes into ten-unit condominiums. People became afraid to loiter, lest they be turned into small condos.

The beaches, managed by the National Seashore, are long and glorious. They stabilized the shifting sand dunes in a five-year program of beach grass planting that in its early years made the dunes look like William Proxmire's hair plugs. The National Seashore fought off development so effectively that many vantage points on the beach still offer views unobstructed by anything man-made. But, while their nature management skills are commendable, they have the people skills of Josef Mengele and have managed to antagonize the locals with their rules about dogs on leashes, people on paths, and suits on sunbathers.

One of the tasks the National Seashore takes most seriously is its summer-long patrolling of nude sunbathers. There's a job. What is the civil service qualifying test like? "Can spot a naked breast at fifty paces."

Bathers watch out for each other and periodic warning shouts of "Tit patrol!" ring out over the sun-drenched dunes.

Locals and those otherwise in the know drive their four-wheel-drive vehicles out onto the beach to the tidal pools unreachable by the casual walker and have all-day tailgate picnics and beach fires.

Although the beaches are long and expansive, edged with sea oats and beach plum, gay people congregate on a tiny strip of land at Herring Cove Beach. Five winters of nor'easters have eroded beaches so much that a high tide on an August afternoon forces hundreds onto a beach the size of a commemorative stamp.

Lesbians tend to stay at the entrance to the beach with their blankets, beach chairs, coolers, umbrellas, radios, jarts, and inflatable floating devices in the shapes of Puff the Magic Dragon or Xena, Warrior Princess. The lesbians stay there, because it is a known fact that lesbians don't like to carry stuff. On occasion I have had the misfortune of going to the beach with a woman who has participated in a Lesbian Outward Bound program and has something to prove, so she drags her worldly possessions for miles down the beach. But more often I've been with lesbians who get out of the car in the parking lot, look around, and say, "This looks good to me."

The area between the gay men's section and the lesbians section, known as the DMZ, has been growing over the years, especially in the coparenting gay baby boom. Well-oiled gay fathers stand at the edge of the water shouting, "Sophie Flanagan-Roth, that's too far out!"

Other gay men walk a long way down the beach, carrying a six-ounce bottle of Evian, wearing nothing but a butt thong. It's a fabulous parade. I saw one gay man who pivoted so much on the balls of his feet that it was a miracle he made any forward motion. If he made one wrong move, it was a 360° right into the sand, a homo roto rooter, fine for installing fence posts, but no way to walk down the beach.

One almost mandatory activity for visitors to Provincetown is the whale watch. The *Portuguese Princess* ferries watchers an hour out of the harbor, past lighthouses and beaches while Coastal Studies personnel narrate nonstop like some Discovery Channellers run amok.

Labor Day signals the end of the most manic tourist and traffic season and for a few months the pace of the town ratchets down a notch or two and caters to speciality weekends. Women's Week sponsored by the women innkeepers draws thousands of lesbians from all over the Northeast, many with the same haircuts. Split level: short on the top, short on the sides, long in the back.

Some years scheduling snafus have caused Women's Week to overlap with Fantasia Faire, the oldest and largest convention of cross-dressers in the country. Known fondly to townies as "The Tall Women," they are straight men in the world's largest Aerosoles, attended by their understanding, long-suffering, wives. They attend seminars on makeup and accessories, have talent shows, luncheons, even proms. Rainy days are an opportunity to trot out the largest collection of belted London Fog raincoats and mesh rainhats since Adlai Stevenson's funeral. Meantime, tour buses daily disgorge packs of senior citizens who come to Provincetown "to see the foliage."

After Halloween and the beginning of daylight saving time, the sun sets at four and the town becomes a petri dish of a community struggling to get along. Gay and straight, townies and washashores struggle with each other over issues of septic systems, schools, road maintenance, and waste disposal.

It is a work in progress and open for all to see at the yearly town meeting in the old wooden balconied Town Hall. It looks like the courtroom scene from *To Kill a Mockingbird*. For five or seven or however many nights are needed, every registered voter in town is eligible to vote on motions openly and endlessly debated in one of the oldest extant town meetings in New England.

Before moving to Provincetown permanently, I worked there doing stand-up for longer periods of time each summer—ten days, then two weeks, then three weeks—always in August. After Labor Day one year, I was packing to move back to upstate New York and sadly thought, "Why? Why now when it's so beautiful and the tourists have all gone home?" So I stayed. I found a six-month rental on the water and in October began the Provincetown shuffle, predictable as the tides, living six months off-season on the water and then moving inland in May for six months during the season.

This mobility is a very old Provincetown tradition dating back to its sea captains who thought of houses in the same mobile way that they thought of their ships. Some house moving was conditioned by shifting dunes. But in most cases, captains just moved their houses every spring, propped them up on rollers and had them dragged by horses to a new location.

One captain moved his newly widowed mother and her house to the yard behind his house so he could be closer to her. When she became ill, he had her house moved down the hill and attached to his house. When she died, the sight of her house made him so sad that he had it moved up the hill again.

Since I rented apartments in Provincetown for three years and seven moves, I knew when a good deal on a house came along. The house I bought is in an old Portuguese neighborhood, an area that used to be a pig farm, so the soil is rich like the gardens of Findhorn. Pig Acres was where chauffeurs kept their cars and the hired help lived.

In newer neighborhoods, roads cut into fragile sand dunes are named Pilgrim Heights, Standish Way, and We Were Here First Lane. We, in the old Portuguese section, call ourselves Linguica Gardens, and unlike other transient, rental sections of town, we are here to stay. The couple across the way celebrated their fiftieth wedding anniversary recently. Two sisters, Genevieve and Kitty, aged eighty-nine and ninety-one, live in the corner house. They walk into town every day, slowly, with frequent stops on benches or stoops. They don't see well, both wear wraparound postcataract operation sun goggles over their glasses; one favors yellow, the other, dark brown. But they switch sometimes so I am never sure who is who. The two of them come up close to me, peck me in the plexus with their gnarly forefingers, and say, "Now which one are you?"

Peter and Rita, together forty-two years, live next door.

One August morning in 1992, as I was rushing out my gate I was intercepted by Peter in his mesh cap and belted navy blue, one-piece yard-work uniform. He huffed to catch up with me.

"Didja hear that fight last night?"

"No. Where was it?"

He indicated with a discreet nod of the head: "Next door."

I said, "I have never heard them fight."

"Oh dahlin, they were goin' at it, callin' each other f . . . in' liar, f . . . in' this 'n' that, every name in the book."

"Are you sure? What time?"

"Had to be ten o'clock, ten-fifteen."

Then it dawned on me. "Oh Peter! It wasn't them!

It was us! We were watching the Republican convention, screaming at George Bush during his speech. We had the windows open. Sorry."

He waddled away. "I agree, dahlin'."

When I first looked for a house, I wanted a two-family home so that someone could watch my place when I was on the road. When I told people in town that I bought a single-family house, and that I was worried about my absences, they said not to worry, everybody'll be watching. They were right.

One late night when I pulled into my parking spot after a two-week road trip, I closed the gate behind me. As I walked down the path to my house, I heard Peter, who was watching baseball on his bedroom TV, say to Rita, watching her program in the living room, "Kate's home."

vindiKate

---

1. v. we shall overcome, and then who knows what we'll do.

It was 7:00 A.M. in the tiny soundproofed room. My interviewer swung the microphone to his mouth, and on the OK cue from his producer, leaned in chummily and purred, "I love your music."

I leaned into my microphone, ducktaped to the wire-hanger-as-overhead-boom, and said, "You hear it too?"

He had just done the morning drivetime report, meaningless for the town of five thousand, and had my bio material on the table in front of him with nary a highlighted mark on it. He must have attended a Communications lecture about putting an interviewee at ease. Preparation also helps.

When I first started performing, I called myself a "fumerist," a neologism combining feminist and humorist, suggesting anger, fuming, flaming, spontaneous

no idea of the courage it took every lesbian there to get to that audience.

After the standard thanks-for-coming-out opening, the show is like a newspaper, a gay *USA Today*, with the news of the day, local to international, style, sports, media, religion, money, science, with editorializing throughout. No matter how much the material changes, two things have stayed the same over the years. The bookends of the show are the welcome and the send-off, the hello, good-bye. While the beginning has never varied, the ending has changed over the years. But the point of it is an adieu, a little pat on the butt, now go on out there, be safe, but raise some hell.

The endings run together like the symphony that will not end. Here are some of my favorites.

We can learn from football. Especially that old double reverse. To take insults as invitations. "You castrating, ball-busting bitch." Well, okay if you insist.

To take warnings as welcomes:

Don't laugh; it only encourages her.

Don't make light.

Make light. Light enough to see where we are going. Light enough to move—after all, this is a woman's movement.

Don't make waves.

Make waves! Take the slide down that big turquoise water slide called life. Be bold. But most of all, be bad.

I came out to my best friend, a straight friend, who is now an ex-friend. It happens, but we get better best friends and we move on.

When I came out to her, she said very sneeringly, "Well, you certainly have made a commitment to joy in your life." And at first I denied it, "Oh no, no, no I haven't. No joy for me in my Mudville."

But then I stopped myself and said, "You know you're right. I have made a commitment to joy in my life and she is not an easy woman to please. Practice. Practice."

Another friend told me that each morning when we get up we have to decide whether we are going to save or savor the world. I don't think that is the decision. It's not an either/or, save or savor. We have to do both, save and savor the world. It's a world that would like to gentrify the wildness of our souls.

In the middle of the gay nineties, the big talk among some gay people was that it was time for us to take our legitimate place at the table. The door to the big house had been kicked in by radical gay activists, and through the door walked the biggest pile of conservatives you ever saw, all yelling at the people who kicked in the doors for behaving poorly. They wanted a place at the table. Say thank you for the crumbs and the sound bites, snacks full of empty calories.

The highly visible door-kickers were told by the recently invisible that they had to learn how to compromise, to play politics, to grow up—till I wanted to throw up. The virtually normal wanted gay people to be part of the mainstream. Their motto: "If I can't whine, it's not my revolution."

Weakened dykes are always blamed for catastrophes. Let me close with a quote from the longtime activist, writer teacher, Grace Paley: "The mainstream is wide and shallow and slow moving. It's the tributaries where the fun is."

Since the goal of feminism is the end of the oppression of women and since there still seem to be some loose ends to tie up before we bring it about, I will be employed as a feminist humorist for a few more years. No downsizing, no layoffs, no early retirement packages for me. Obsolescence is my plan. Liberation is the goal.

About the Author

A self-described fumerist (feminist/humorist), KATE CLINTON taught English for eight years before a writing workshop and improvisational class convinced her that her political views deserved a public hearing. She quit teaching, took a job as a window washer, and started her professional stand-up career in 1981. She performs one-woman shows across the country and writes columns for *The Progressive* and *The Advocate*. She has appeared on *Oprah*, *Arsenio Hall*, *Good Morning America*, *Nightline*, CNN, *Entertainment Tonight*, and many other programs. Although she has four comedy albums to her credit, *Don't Get Me Started* is her first book.